The Renascence of Hebrew Literature (1743-1885)

Nahum Slouschz

Contents

INTRODUCTION	7
CHAPTER I	12
CHAPTER II	18
CHAPTER III	30
CHAPTER IV	54
CHAPTER V	71
CHAPTER VI	91
CHAPTER VII	98
CHAPTER VIII	120
CHAPTER IX	130
CHAPTER X	137
CHAPTER XI	143
CHAPTER XII	158
CONCLUSION	165

THE RENASCENCE OF
HEBREW LITERATURE
(1743-1885)

BY

Nahum Slouschz

INTRODUCTION

It was long believed that Hebrew had no place among the modern languages as a literary vehicle. The circumstance that the Jews of Western countries had given up the use of their national language outside of the synagogue was not calculated to discredit the belief. The Hebrew, it was generally held, had once been alive, but now it belonged among the dead languages, in the same sense as the Greek and the Latin. And when from time to time some new work in Hebrew, or even a periodical publication, reached a library, the cataloguer classified it with theologic and Rabbinic treatises, without taking the trouble to obtain information as to the subject of the book or the purpose of the journal. In point of fact, in the large majority of cases they were far enough removed from Rabbinic controversy.

Sometimes it happened that one or another Hebraist was overcome with astonishment at the sight of a Hebrew translation of a modern author. And he stopped at that. He never went so far as to enable himself to pass judgment upon it from the critical or the literary point of view. To what purpose? he would ask himself. Hebrew has been dead these many centuries, and to use it is an anachronism. He considered it only a curiosity of literature, literary sleight of hand, nothing more.

The bare possibility of the existence of a modern literature in Hebrew seemed so strange, so improbable, that the best-informed circles refused to entertain the notion seriously--perhaps not without some semblance of a reason for their incredulity.

The history of the development of modern Hebrew literature, its character, the extraordinary conditions fostering it, its very existence, are of a sort to surprise one who has not kept in touch with the internal struggles, the intellectual currents that have agitated the Judaism of Eastern Europe in the course of the past century.

So far from deserving a reputation for casuistry, modern Hebrew literature is, if anything, distinctly rationalistic in character. It is anti-dogmatic and anti-Rabbinic. Its avowed aim is to enlighten the Jewish masses that have remained faithful to religious tradition, and to interpenetrate the Jewish communities with the conceptions of modern life.

Since the French Revolution the ghetto has produced valiant champions of every good cause, politicians, legislators, poets, who have taken part in all the movements of their day. But it has also given birth to a legion of men of action sprung from the people and remaining with the people, who, in the name of liberty of conscience and in the name of science, fought the same battles upon the field of traditional Judaism that the others were fighting outside.

A whole school of literary humanists undertook the work of emancipating the Jewish masses, and pursued it for several generations with admirable zeal. Hebrew became an excellent instrument of propaganda in their hands. Thanks to their efforts, the language of the prophets, inarticulate for nearly two thousand years, was developed to a striking degree of perfection. It was shown to be a flexible medium, varied enough to serve as the vehicle for any modern idea.

The great wonder is that this modern literature in Hebrew made itself without teachers, without patrons, without academies and literary ***salons***, without encouragement in any shape or form. Nor is that all. It was impeded by inconceivable obstacles, ranging from the fraudulence of an absurd censorship to the persecution of fanatics. In such circumstances, only the purest idealism, and the most disinterested, could have ventured to enter the lists, and could have come off the victor.

While the emancipated Jew of the Occident replaced Hebrew by the vernacular of his adopted country; while the Rabbis were distrustful of whatever is not religion; and rich patrons refused to support a literature that had not the ***entree*** of good society,--while these held aloof, the ***Maskil*** ("the intellectual") of the small provincial town, the Polish vagabond ***Mehabber*** ("author"), despised and unknown, often a martyr to his conviction, who devoted himself heart, soul, and might to maintaining honorably the literary traditions of Hebrew,--he alone remained faithful to what has been the true mission of the Bible language since its beginnings.

It is a renewal of the ancient literary impulse of the humble, the disinherited, whence first sprang the Bible. It is a repetition of the phenomenon of the popular prophet-orators, reappearing in modern Hebrew garb.

The Renascence of Hebrew Literature (1743-1885)

The return to the language and the ideas of an eventful past marks a decisive stage in the perturbed career of the Jewish people. It indicates the re-awakening of national feeling.

The history of modern Hebrew literature thus forms an extremely instructive page in the history of the Jewish people. It is especially interesting from the point of view of social psychology, furnishing, as it does, valuable documents upon the course taken by new ideas in impregnating surroundings that are characteristically obdurate toward intellectual suggestions from without. The century-long struggle between free-thinking and blind faith, between common sense and absurdity consecrated by age and exalted by suffering, reveals an intense social life, a continual clashing of ideas and sentiments.

It is a literature that offers us the grievous spectacle of poets and writers who are constantly expressing their anxiety lest it disappear with them, and yet devote themselves unremittingly to its cultivation, with all the ardor of despair. At their side, however, we see optimistic dreamers, worthy disciples of the prophets. In the midst of the ruin of all that made the past glorious, and in the face of the downfall of cherished hopes, they lose not an iota of their faith in the future of their people, in its speedy regeneration.

What we have before us is the issue of the supreme internal struggle that engaged the great masses of the Jews torn from their moorings by the disquietude of modern existence. A fervent desire for a better social life took possession of all minds. The conviction that the eternal people cannot disappear seems to have regained ground and to have been stronger than ever, and the current again set in the direction of auto-emancipation.

It is the true literature of the Jewish people that we are called upon to examine, the product of the ghetto, the reflex of its psychic states, the expression of its misery, its suffering, and also its hope. The people of the Bible is not dead, and in its very own language we must seek the true Jewish spirit, the national soul.

Let not the reader expect to find perfection of form, pure art, in its often monotonous lyric poetry, or its prolix, didactic novels. The authors of the ghetto felt too much, suffered too much, were too much under the dominance of a life of misery, a semi-Asiatic, semi-mediaeval ***regime***, to have had heart for the cultivation of mere form. Does the Song of Songs fall short of being a literary document of the first order because it does not equal the dramas of Euripides in artistic completeness? It is conceded that the proper aim of the artist is art, finished and perfect art, but to the philosopher, the social investigator, the important thing is the advance of ideas.

* * * * *

The object of the writer in presenting this essay to the public was not to presume to give a detailed exposition of the development of modern Hebrew literature, accomplishing itself under the most complex of social and political conditions and in a social *milieu* totally unknown to the public at large. That would have led too far. It was not even possible to give an adequate idea of all the authors requiring mention within the limited frame adopted perforce. Besides, nothing or almost nothing existed in the way of monographs that might have facilitated the task. [In point of fact, all that can be cited are the following: the admirable biographical essays on Mapu, Smolenskin, etc., by Reuben Brainin; those of S. Bernfeld on Rapoport, etc., these two critics writing in Hebrew; and the sketch of our subject by M. Klausner, in the Russian language. Besides, mention may be made of an article in the **Revue des Revues**, by M. Ludvipol, of Paris. In spite of the diversity of schools and the conditions giving rise to them, which are here to be treated for the first time from the point of view of a modern history of literature, the reader will readily convince himself that the subject lacks neither coherence nor unity. It is superfluous to say that in this first attempt at a history of modern Hebrew literature, the grouping of movements and schools borrowed from the Occidental literatures is bound to have only relative value.]

The aim set up by the present writer is merely to follow up the various stages through which modern Hebrew literature has passed, to deduce and specify the general principles that have moulded it, and analyze the literary and social value of the works produced by the representative writers of the epoch embraced.

In a word, the object is to show how Hebrew poetry was emancipated from the tradition of the Middle Ages under the influence of the Italian humanists, how it underwent a process of modernization, and served as the model for a literary renascence in Germany and Austria. [Especially Moses Hayyim Luzzatto, in his "Glory to the Righteous", published in 1743, which has been made the point of departure in the present inquiry.] In these two countries Hebrew letters were enriched and perfected from the point of view of form as well as content. Finally, due to favorable circumstances, the Hebrew language captured its place as the literary and national language among the Jews of Poland, and particularly of Lithuania.

In this progress eastward, Hebrew literature has never been faithless to its mission. Two currents of ideas, more or less distinct, characterize it. On the one hand is the intellectual emancipation of the Jewish masses, which had fallen into ignorance, and, as a consequence, the conflict with prejudice and Rabbinic dogmatism; and, on the other hand, the awakening of national sentiment and Jewish solidarity. These two currents of ideas finally flow together in contemporaneous literature, in the creation of the national Jewish movement in its various modifications. During a period of about twenty years, since 1882, the course of events has forced the national emancipation of the Jewish masses upon their educated leaders. By the same token, Hebrew has been assigned a dominating position in all vital questions agitating Judaism, and there has been brought about a literary development that is truly significant.

CHAPTER I
IN ITALY
MOSES HAYYIM LUZZATTO

In its precise sense, the term Renascence cannot be applied to the movement that asserted itself in Hebrew literature at the end of the fifteenth century, as little as the term Decadence can be applied to the epoch preceding it.

Long before Dante and Boccaccio, as far back as the eleventh century, Hebrew literature, particularly in Spain, and to a certain extent also in the Provence, had reached a degree of development unknown in European languages during the Middle Ages.

Though the persecutions toward the end of the fourteenth and the fifteenth century crushed the Jewish communities in Spain and in the Provence, they yet did not succeed in annihilating completely the intellectual traditions of the Spanish and French Jews. Remnants of Jewish science and Jewish literature were carried by the refugees into the countries of their adoption, and in the Netherlands, in Turkey, even in Palestine, schools were founded after a short interval.

But a literary revival was possible only in Italy. Elsewhere, in the backward countries of the North and the East, the Jews, smarting from blows recently inflicted, withdrew within themselves. They took refuge in the most sombre of mysticisms, or, at least, in dogmatism of the narrowest kind. The Italian Jewish communities, thanks to the more bearable conditions prevailing around them, were in a position to carry on the literary traditions of Jewish Spain. In Italy thinkers arose, and writers, and poets. There was Azariah dei Rossi, the father of historical criticism; Messer Leon, the subtle philosopher; Elijah Levita, the grammarian; Leon of Modena, the keen-witted rationalist; Joseph Delmedigo, of encyclopedic mind; the

The Renascence of Hebrew Literature (1743-1885)

Frances brothers, both poets, who combated mysticism; and many others too numerous to mention. [For the greater part of these writers, see Gustav Karpeles, ***Geschichte der judischen Literatur***, 2 vols., Berlin, 1886.] These, together with a few stray writers in Turkey and the Netherlands, imparted a certain degree of distinction to the Hebrew literature of the sixteenth and the seventeenth century. Heirs to the Spanish traditions, they nevertheless were inclined to oppose the spirit and particularly the rules of Arabic prosody, which had put manacles upon Hebrew poetry. Their efforts were directed to the end of introducing new literary forms and new concepts into Hebrew literature.

They did not meet with notable success. The greater number of Jewish men of letters, whose knowledge of foreign literatures was meagre, were destined to remain in the thrall of the Middle Ages until a much later time. As to the unlettered, they preferred to make use of the vernacular, which presented fewer difficulties than the Hebrew.

The task of tearing asunder the chains that hampered the evolution of Hebrew in a modern sense devolved upon an Italian Jew of amazing talent. He became the true, the sovereign inaugurator of the Hebrew Renascence.

Moses Hayyim Luzzatto was born at Padua, in 1707. He was descended from a family celebrated for the Rabbinic scholars and the writers it had given to Judaism, a celebrity which it has continued to earn for itself down to our own day.

His education was strictly Rabbinic, consisting chiefly of the study of the Talmud, under the direction of a Polish teacher, for the Polish Rabbis had attained to a position of great esteem as early as Luzzatto's day. He lost little time in initiating his pupil into the mysteries of the Kabbalah, and so the early childhood years of our poet were a sad time spent in the stifling atmosphere of the ghetto. Happily for him, it was an Italian ghetto, whence secular learning had not been banished completely.

While pursuing his religious studies, the child became acquainted with the Hebrew poetry of the Middle Ages and with the Italian literature of his own time. In the latter accomplishment lies his superiority to the Hebrew scholars of other countries, who were shut off from every outside influence, and held fast to obsolete forms and ideas.

From early youth Luzzatto showed remarkable aptitude for poetry. At the age of seventeen he composed a drama in verse entitled "Samson and Delilah". A little later he published a work on prosody, **_Leshon Limmudim_** ("The Language of Learners", Mantua, 1727), and dedicated it to his Polish teacher. The young man then decided to break with the poetry of the Middle Ages, which hampered the development of the Hebrew language. His allegorical drama, **_Migdal 'Oz_** ("The Tower of Victory"), inspired by the **_Pastor fido_** of Guarini, was the first token of this reform. Its style is marked by an elegance and vividness not attained since the close of the Bible. [Though it was widely circulated in manuscript, **_Migdal 'Oz_** did not appear in print until 1837, at Leipsic, edited by M. H. Letteris.] In spite of its prolixity and the absence of all dramatic action, it continues to this day to make its appeal to the fancy of the literary. A poetic breath animates it, and it is characterized by the artistic taste that is one of the distinctions of its author.

It was a new world that **_Migdal 'Oz_**, by its laudation of rural life, disclosed to the votaries of a literature the most enlightened representatives of which refused to see in the Song of Songs anything but religious symbolism, so far had their appreciation of reality and nature degenerated.

In imitation of the pastorals of his time, though it may be with more genuine feeling, Luzzatto sings the praises of the shepherd's life:

> "How beautiful, how sweet, is the lot of the young shepherd of flocks! Between the folds he leads his sheep, now walking, now running hither and thither. Poor though he is, he is full of joy. His countenance reflects the gladness of his heart. In the shade of trees he reposes, and apprehends no danger. Poor though he is, yet he is happy....
>
> "The maiden who charms his eyes, and attracts his desire, in whom his heart has pleasure, returns his affection with responsive gladness. They know naught but delight--neither separation nor obstacle affrights them. They sport together, they enjoy their happiness, with none to disturb. When weariness steals over him, he forgets his toil on her bosom; the light of her countenance swiftly banishes all thought of his travail. Poor though he is,

yet he is happy!" (Act III, scene I.)

Alas, this call to a more natural life, after centuries of physical degeneration and suppression of all feeling for nature, could not be understood, nor even taken seriously, in surroundings in which air, sunlight, the very right to live, had been refused or measured out penuriously. The drama remained in manuscript, and did not become known to the public at large.

It was Luzzatto's chief work that exercised decisive influence on the development of Hebrew literature. ***La-Yesharim Tehillah*** ("Glory to the Righteous"), another allegorical drama, which appeared in 1743, is considered a model of its kind until this day. It introduced a new epoch, the modern epoch, in the history of Hebrew literature. The master stands revealed by every touch. Everything betrays his skill--the style, at once elegant, significant, and precise, recalling the pure style of the Bible, the fresh and glowing figures of speech, the original poetic inspiration, and the thought, which bears the imprint of a profound philosophy and a high moral sense, and is free from all trace of mystical exaggeration.

From the point of view of dramatic art, the piece is not of the highest interest. The subject, purely moral and didactic, gives no opportunity for a serious study of character, and, as in all allegorical pieces, the dramatic action is weak.

The theme was not new. Even in Hebrew and before Luzzatto, it had been treated several times. It is the struggle between Justice and Injustice, between Truth and Falsehood. The allegorical personages who take part in the action are, arrayed on one side, Yosher (Righteousness) aided by Sekel (Reason) and Mishpat (Justice), and, on the other side, Sheker (Falsehood) and her auxiliaries, Tarmit (Deceit), Dimyon (Imagination), and Taawah (Passion). The two hostile camps strive together for the favor of the beautiful maiden Tehillah (Glory), the daughter of Hamon (the Crowd). The struggle is unequal. Imagination and Passion carry the day in the face of Truth and Righteousness. Then the inevitable ***deus ex machina***, in this case God Himself, intervenes, and Justice is again enthroned.

This simple and not strikingly original frame encloses beautiful descriptions of nature and, above all, sublime thoughts, which make the piece one of the gems of Hebrew poetry. The predominant idea of the book is to glorify God and admire the "innumerable wonders of the Creator."

"All who seek will find them, in every living being, in every
plant, in every lifeless object, in all things on earth and in
the sea, in whatsoever the human eye rests upon. Happy he who
hath found knowledge and wisdom, happy he if their speech hath
fallen upon an attentive ear!" (Act II, scene I.)

But the Creator is not capricious. Reason and Truth are His attributes, and they appear in all His acts. Humanity is a mob, and two opposing forces contend for the mastery over it: Truth with Righteousness on one side, Falsehood and her ilk on the other. Each of these two forces seeks to rule the crowd and prevail in triumph.

The Reason personified by the poet has nothing in common with the positive Reason of the rationalists, which takes the world to be directed by mechanical and immutable laws. It is supreme Reason, obeying moral laws too sublimated for our powers of appreciation. How could it be otherwise? Are we not the continual plaything of our senses, which are incapable of grasping absolute truths, and deceive us even about the appearance of things?

"Truly, our eyes are deluded, for eyes of flesh they are.
Therefore they change truth into falsehood, darkness they make
light, and light darkness. Lo, a small chance, a mere accident,
suffices to distort our view of tangible things; how much more do
we stray from the truth with things beyond the reach of our
senses? See the oars in the water. They seem crooked and twisted.
Yet we know them to be straight....

"Verily, man's heart is like the ocean ceaselessly agitated by
the battling winds. As the waves roll forward and backward in
perpetual motion, so our hearts are stirred by never-ending pain
and trouble, and as our emotions sway our will, so our senses
suffer change within us. We see only what we desire to see, hear
only what we long to hear, what our imagination conjures up."
(Act II, scene i.)

This philosophy of externalism and of the impotence of the human mind threw the poet, believer and devotee of the Kabbalah, into a most dangerous mysticism. He continued to write for some time: an imitation of the Psalms; a treatise on logic, **Ha-Higgayon**, not without value; another treatise on ethics, **Mesilat Yesharim** ("The Path of the Righteous"); and a large number of poetic pieces and Kabbalistic compositions, the greater part of which were never published; and this enumeration does not exhaust the tale of his literary achievements. [The greater part of Luzzatto's works have never been published.] Then his powers were used up, the tension of his mind increased to the last degree; he lost his moral equilibrium. The day came when he strayed so far afield as to believe himself called to play the role of the Messiah. The Rabbis, alarmed at the gloomy prospect of a repetition of the pseudo-Messianic movements which time and again had shaken the Jewish world to its foundations, launched the ban against him. His fate was sealed by his ingenious imitation of the Zohar, written in Aramaic, of which only fragments have been preserved. Obliged to leave Italy, Luzzatto wandered through Germany, and took up his abode at Amsterdam. He enjoyed the gratification of being welcomed there by literary men among his people as a veritable master. At Amsterdam he wrote his last works. But he did not remain there long. He went to seek Divine inspiration at Safed in Palestine, the far-famed centre of the Kabbalah. There he died, cut off by the plague at the age of forty.

Such was the sad life of the poet, a victim of the abnormal surroundings in which he lived. Under more favorable conditions, he might have achieved that which would have won him universal recognition. His main distinction is that he released the Hebrew language forever from the forms and ideas of the Middle Ages, and connected it with the circle of modern literatures. He bequeathed to posterity a model of classic poetry, which ushered in Hebrew humanism, the return to the style and the manner of the Bible, in the same way as the general humanistic movement led the European mind back upon its own steps along the paths marked out by the classic languages. No sooner did his work become known in the north countries and in the Orient than it raised up imitators. Mendes and Wessely, leaders of literary revivals, the one at Amsterdam, the other in Germany, are but the disciples and successors of the Italian poet.

CHAPTER II
IN GERMANY
THE MEASSEFIM

The intellectual emancipation of the Jews in Germany anticipated their political and social emancipation. That is a truth generally acknowledged. Long secluded from all foreign ideas, confined within religious and dogmatic bounds, German Judaism was a sharer in the physical and social misery of the Judaism of Slavic countries. The philosophic and tolerant ideas in vogue at the end of the eighteenth century startled it somewhat out of its torpor. In the measure in which those ideas gained a foothold in the communities, conditions, at least in the larger centres, took on a comfortable aspect, with more or less assurance of permanent well-being. The first contact of the ghetto with the enlightened circles of the day gave the impetus to a marked movement toward an inner emancipation. Associations of **Maskilim** ("intellectuals") were formed at Berlin, Hamburg, and Breslau. "The Seekers of the Good and the Noble" (**Shohare ha-Tob weha-Tushiyah**) should be mentioned particularly. They were composed of educated men familiar with Occidental culture, and animated by the desire to make the light of that culture penetrate to the heart of the provincial communities. These "intellectuals" entered the lists against religious fanaticism and casuistic methods, seeking to replace them by liberal ideas and scientific research. Two schools, headed respectively by the philosopher Mendelssohn and the poet Wessely, had their origin in this movement--the school of the **Biurists**, deriving their name from the **Biur**, a commentary on the Bible, and the school of the **Meassefim**, from **Meassef**, "Collector." [A specimen of the **Biur** appeared at Amsterdam, in 1778, under the title **'Alim le-Terufah**.] The former defended Judaism against the enemies from without, and combated the prejudices and the ignorance of the Jews themselves. The Meassefim took as their sphere of activity the reform of the education of the young and the revival of the Hebrew language. The two schools agreed that to elevate the moral and social status of the Jews, it was necessary to remove first the external peculiarities separating them from their fellow-citizens. A new translation of the Bible into literary German, undertaken by Mendelssohn, was to deal the death blow to the Jewish-German (*judisch-deutsch*) jargon, and the **Biur**, the commentary on the Bible mentioned above, produced by the co-operation of a galaxy of scholars and men of culture, was expected to sweep aside all mystic and allegoric interpretations of the Scriptures and introduce the rational and scientific method.

The results achieved by the Biurists tended beyond a doubt toward the elevation of the mass of the Jews. One of these results was, as had been hoped for, the dislodgment of the Jewish-German by the spread of the pure German. The influence wielded by the Biurists, so far from stopping with the German Jews, extended to the Jewish communities of Eastern Europe.

*　*　*　*　*

In 1784-5, two Hebrew writers, Isaac Euchel and Mendel Bresslau, undertook to publish a magazine, entitled **Ha-Meassef** ("The Collector"), whence the name Meassefim. The enterprise was under the auspices of Mendelssohn and Wessely. A double aim was to be served. The periodical was to promote the spread of knowledge and modern ideas in the Hebrew language, the only language available for the Jews of the ghetto; and at the same time it was to promote the purification of Hebrew, which had degenerated in the Rabbinical schools. Its readers were to be familiarized with the social and aesthetic demands of modern life, and induced to rid themselves of ingrained peculiarities. Besides its success in these directions, it must be set to the credit of **Ha- Meassef**, that it was the first agency to gather under one banner all the champions of the **Haskalah** in the several countries of Europe. It supplied the link connecting them with one another. [Properly speaking, the term Haskalah includes the notion at once of humanism and humanitarianism.]

From the literary point of view ***Ha-Meassef*** is of subordinate interest. Its contributors were devoid of taste. They offered their readers mainly questionable imitations of the works of the German romantic school. The periodical brought no new talent truly worthy of the description into notice. Whatever reputation its principal writers enjoyed had been won before the appearance of ***Ha-Meassef***. They owed their fame primarily to the favor acquired for Hebrew letters through the efforts of Luzzatto's disciples. [Since the appearance of ***La-Yesharim Tehillah*** by Luzzatto, imitations of it without number have been published, and for the eighteenth century alone allegorical dramas by the dozen might be enumerated.] Of the poems published in ***Ha-Meassef*** but a few deserve notice, and even they are nothing more than mediocre imitations of didactic pieces in the style of the day, or odes celebrating the splendor of contemporary kings and princes. A poem by Wessely forms a rare exception. It extols the residents of Basle, who, in 1789, welcomed Jewish refugees from Alsace. And if we turn from its poetry to its historical contributions, we find that the biographies, as of Abarbanel and Joseph Delmedigo, are hardly scientific; they occupy themselves with external facts to the neglect of underlying ideas. On the whole, ***Ha-Meassef*** was an engine of propaganda and polemics rather than a literary production, though the campaign carried on in its pages against straitlaced orthodoxy and the Rabbis did not reach the degree of bitterness which was to characterize later periods--moderation that was due to its most prominent contributors. Wessely exhorted the editors not to attack religiousness nor ridicule the Rabbis, and Mendelssohn devoted his articles to minor points of Rabbinic practice, such as the permissibility of vaccination under the Jewish law.

The French Revolution precipitated events in an unexpected way. The tone of ***Ha-Meassef*** changed. It held that knowledge and liberty alone could save the Jews. More aggressive toward the Rabbis than before, it attacked fanaticism, and gave space to trite poems, glorifying a life, for instance, in which women and wine played the prominent part (1790). Six years after its first issue, ***Ha-Meassef*** ceased to appear, not without having materially advanced the intellectual emancipation of the German Jews and the revival of Hebrew as a secular language. [The first series of ***Ha-Meassef*** ran from 1784-1786 (Konigsberg), and from 1788-1790 (Konigsberg and Berlin). An additional volume began to appear in 1794, at Berlin and Breslau, under the editorship of Lowe and Wolfsohn, and was completed in 1797. The second series ran from 1809 to 1811 at Berlin, Altona, and Dessau, under Shalom Hacohen. [Trl.]] So important was this first co-operative enterprise in Hebrew letters, that it imposed its name on the whole of the literary movement of the second half of the eighteenth century, the epoch of the Meassefim.

Two poets and five or six prose writers more or less worthy of the name of author dominated the period.

Naphtali Hartwig Wessely (born at Hamburg in 1725; died there in 1805) is considered the prince of the poets of the time. Belonging to a rather intelligent family in easy circumstances, he received a modern education. Though his mind was open to all the new influences, he nevertheless remained a loyal adherent of his faith, and occupied strictly religious ground until the end. He devoted himself with success to the cultivation of poetry, and completed the work of reform begun by the Italian Luzzatto, to whom, however, he was inferior in depth and originality.

Wessely's poetic masterpiece was **Shire Tiferet** ("Songs of Glory"), or the Epic of Moses (Berlin, 1789), in five volumes. This poem of the Exodus is on the model of the pseudo-classic productions of the Germany of his day; the influence of Klopstock's **Messias**, for instance, is striking.

Depth of thought, feeling for art, and original poetic imagination are lacking in **Shire Tiferet**. Practically it is nothing more than an oratorical paraphrase of the Biblical recital. The shortcomings of his main work are characteristic of all the poetry by Wessely. On the other hand, his oratorical manner is unusually attractive, and his Hebrew is elegant and chaste. The somewhat labored precision of his style, taken together with the absence of the poetic temperament, makes of him the Malherbe of modern Hebrew poetry. He enjoyed the love and admiration of his contemporaries to an extraordinary degree, and his chief poem underwent a large number of editions, becoming in course of time a popular book, and regarded with kindly favor even by the most orthodox-- testimony at once to the poet's personal influence upon his co- religionists and the growing importance of the Hebrew language.

Wessely wrote also several important works on questions in Hebrew grammar and philology. The chief of them is **Lebanon**, two parts of which appeared, each separately, under the title **Gan Na'ul** ("The Locked Garden", Berlin, 1765); the other parts never appeared in print. They bear witness to their author's solid scientific attainments, and it is regrettable that their value is obscured by his style, diffuse to the point of prolixity. Besides, Wessely contributed to the German translation of the Bible, and to the commentary on the Bible, both, as mentioned before, works presided over by Mendelssohn, to whom he was attached by the tie of admiring friendship.

Wessely's chief distinction, however, was his firm character and his love of truth. His high ethical qualities were revealed notably in his pamphlet **Dibre Shalom wa-Emet** ("Words of Peace and Truth," Berlin, 1781), elicited by the edict of Emperor Joseph II ordering a reform of Jewish education and the establishment of modern schools for Jews. Though well on in years, he yet did not shrink from the risk of incurring the anger of the fanatics. He openly declared himself in favor of pedagogic innovations. With sage-like modesty and mildness, the poet stated the pressing need for adopting new educational methods, and showed them to be by no means in opposition to the Mosaic and Rabbinic conception of the Jewish faith. In the name of **Torat ha-Adam**, the law for man as such, he set forth urgent reforms which would raise the prestige of the Law as well as of the Jews. He hoped for civil liberty, the liberty the Jews were enjoying in England and in the Netherlands. However, this courageous course gained for him the ban of the fanatics, the effect of which was mitigated by the intervention of the Italian Rabbis in favor of Wessely. On the other hand, it made him the most prominent member of the Meassefim circle; he was regarded as the master of the Maskilim.

Among the most distinguished of the contributors to **Ha-Meassef** is the second writer acclaimed poet by popular consent. David Franco Mendes (1713-1792) was born at Amsterdam, of a family escaped from the Inquisition. Like most Jews of Spanish origin, his family clung to the Spanish language. He was the friend and disciple, and likewise the imitator, of Moses Hayyim Luzzatto. What was true of Eastern Europe, that the Hebrew language prevailed in the ghetto, and had to be resorted to by all who would reach the Jewish masses, did not apply to the countries of the Romance languages. Here Hebrew had little by little been supplanted by the vernacular. Mendes, who paid veritable worship to Hebrew literature, was distressed to see the object of his devotion scorned by his co-religionists and the productions of the classic age of France preferred to it. In the preface to his tragedy, "Athaliah's Recompense" (**Gemul Athaliah**, Amsterdam, 1770), he set himself the task of demonstrating the superiority of the sacred language to the profane languages. Yet this very tragedy, in spite of its author's protestations, is nothing more than a ***rifacimento*** of Racine's drama, and rather infelicitous at that, though it must be admitted that Mendes' style is of classic purity, and some of his scenes are in a measure characterized by vivacity of action. His other drama, "Judith", also published at Amsterdam, has no greater merit than "Athaliah's Recompense." Besides these dramas, Mendes wrote several biographical sketches of the learned men of the Middle Ages for **Ha-Meassef**.

It were far from the truth to say that Mendes succeeded in rivalling the French and Italian authors whom he set up as models for himself. Nevertheless he was endorsed and admired by the literary men of his time as the heir of Luzzatto.

* * * * *

An enumeration of all the writers and all the scholars who, directly or indirectly, contributed to the work of **Ha-Meassef**, would be wearisome. Only those who are distinguished by some degree of originality will be set down by name.

Rabbi Solomon Pappenheim (1776-1814), of Breslau, was the author of a sentimental elegy, **Arba' Kosot** ("The Four Cups", Berlin, 1790). The poem, inspired by Young's "Night Thoughts," is remarkable for its personal note. In his plaints recalling Job's, this Hebrew Werther mourns the loss, not of his mistress--that would not have been in consonance with the spirit of the ghetto--but of his wife and his three children. The elegy came near being a popular poem. Its vapid sentimentality and its affected and exaggerated style were to exercise a baneful influence upon the following generations. It is the tribute paid by Hebrew literature to the diseased spirit of the age. Pappenheim wrote, besides, on Hebrew philology. His work, **Yeri'ot Shelomoh** ("The Curtains of Solomon"), is an important contribution to the subject.

Shalom Hacohen, the editor of a second series of **Ha-Meassef**, published in 1809-1811 (Berlin, Altona, and Dessau), deserves mention. He won considerable fame by his poems and articles, which appeared in the second series of **Ha-Meassef** and in **Bikkure ha-'Ittim** ("The First Fruits of the Times"), and especially through his historical drama, "Amal and Tirzah" (Rodelheim, 1812). The last, a naively conceived piece of work, is well fitted into its Biblical frame. Hacohen is one of the intermediaries between the German Meassefim and their successors in Poland. [Another writer of the epoch, Hartwig Derenburg, whose son and grandson have brilliantly carried on, in France, the literary and scientific traditions of the family, was the author of a widely-read allegorical drama, **Yoshebe Tebel** ("The Inhabitants of the World", Offenbach, 1789).]

Mendelssohn, the master admired and respected by all, contributed, as was mentioned before, only minor controversial articles to **Ha-Meassef**. His preface to the **Biur** and his commentary on Maimonides' treatise on logic are in good style. His philosophical works, "Jerusalem" and "Phaedon," translated into Hebrew by his disciples, were largely instrumental in giving prevalence to the idea that the Jewish people is a religious community rather than a nation. This circumstance explains the banishment of Hebrew from the synagogue by his less religious followers, such as David Friedlander, and the attacks of Herz Homberg on traditional Judaism in his pamphlet "To the Shepherds of Israel" (**El Ro'e Yisrael**).

The chief editor of **Ha-Meassef**, Isaac Euchel (1756-1804), became known for his polemic articles against the superstitions and obscurantism of the fanatics of the ghetto. Euchel wrote also a biographical sketch of Mendelssohn, which was published at Vienna in 1814.

There were also scientific writers among the Meassefim. Baruch Lindau wrote a treatise on the natural sciences, **Reshit Limmudim** ("The Elements of the Sciences", Brunn, 1788), and Mordecai Gumpel Levisohn, the learned professor at the University of Upsala, was the author of a series of scientific essays in **Ha-Meassef**, which contributed greatly to its success.

Up to the time we are speaking of, Poland had supplied the Jewish people with Rabbis and Talmudists, and when the German Jews became imbued with the new spirit, their Polish brethren did not lag behind. Polish authors are to be found among the Meassefim, and several of them deserve special notice.

Kant's brilliant disciple, the profound thinker Solomon Maimon, published only his exegetical works and his ingenious commentary on Maimonides in Hebrew. Another Polish writer, Solomon Dubno (1735-1813), one of the first to cooperate with Mendelssohn in his **Biur**, was a remarkable grammarian and stylist.

Among other things he wrote an allegorical drama and a number of poetic satires. Of the latter, the "Hymn to Hypocrisy", published in *Bikkure To'elet*, is a finished production.

Judah Ben-Zeeb (1764-1811) published in Berlin a Manual of the Hebrew Language (*Talmud Leshon 'Ibri*), planned on modern lines, a work contributing greatly toward spreading a knowledge of philology and rhetoric among the Jews. His Hebrew-German Dictionary and his Hebrew version of Ben Sira are well known to Hebraists.

Isaac Satanow (1732-1804), a Pole residing at Berlin, was a curious personage, interesting alike for the variety of his productions and the oddity of his mental make-up. He possessed a surprising capacity for assimilation. It was this that enabled him to excel, whether he imitated the style of the Bible or the style of mediaeval authors. Hebrew and Aramaic he handled with the same ingenious skill. All his works he attributed to some ancient author. His collection of Proverbs, bearing the name of the Psalmist Asaph (*Mishle Asaph*, Berlin, 1789 and 1792, in three books), would cut a respectable figure in any literature.

A few specimens of his *Mishle*, or maxims, follow:

"Truth springs from research, justice from intelligence. The
beginning of research is curiosity, its essence is discernment,
and its goal truth and justice" (7: 5, 6).

"On the day of thy birth thou didst weep, and those about thee
were glad. On the day of thy death thou wilt laugh, and those
about thee will sigh. Know then, thou wilt one day be born anew
to rejoice in God, and matter will no longer hinder thee" (15: 5,
6). [A play upon words: *Geshem* in Hebrew means
both "matter" and "rain."]

"Rule thy spirit lest others rule thy body" (24:2).

"Pincers are made by means of pincers; work is helped on by work,
and science by science" (34:23).

"Think not what is sweet to thy palate is sweet to thy neighbor's palate. Not so; for many are the beautiful wives that are hated by their husbands, and many the ill-featured wives that are beloved" (43:6,7).

"Every living being leaves off reproducing itself in its old age; but falsehood plays the harlot even in her decrepitude. The older she grows, the deeper she strikes root in the ground, the more numerous becomes her lying progeny, the further does it spread abroad. Her lovers multiply, and those who pay respect to the old adhere to her, that her name be not wiped from the face of the earth" (42:29-31).

Satanow pleaded for the language of the Mishnah as forming part of the Hebrew linguistic stock, but the moment was not propitious to the reform of the prevailing literary style suggested by him.

On the whole, as was intimated before, the literary movement called forth by the Meassefim produced nothing, or almost nothing, of permanent value. The writers of this school acted the part of pioneers and heralds. Being primarily iconoclasts and reformers, they disappeared, with but few exceptions, as soon as their task was completed and the emancipation of the Jews was an accomplished fact in Western Europe. They survived long enough, however, to see the movement with which they were identified sweep away, along with the traditions of the past, also the Hebrew language, the only relic dear to them, the only Jewish thing capable of awakening a responsive thrill in their hearts.

Passionate humanists, and not very clear-sighted, they permitted themselves to be dazzled by modernity and promises of light and liberty, and forswore the ideal of the re-nationalization of Israel, so placing themselves outside the fellowship bond that united, by a common hope, the great masses of the Jews who were still attached to their faith and to their people.

Writers of no consequence in many cases, and of no originality whatsoever, failing to recognize the grandeur of Israel's past, the Meassefim despised their Jewish surroundings too heartily to seek inspiration in them. For the most part they were shallow imitators, second-rate translators of Schiller and Racine. The language of the Jewish soul they could not speak, and they could not formulate a new ideal to take the place of the tottering traditions of the past and the faltering hope of a Messianic time. An entire generation was to pass before historical Judaism came into its own again, through the creation of a pure "Science of Judaism" and the conception of the mission of the Jewish people.

Nevertheless the movement called into being by the Meassefim caused considerable stir. For the first time the Rabbinic tradition, petrified by age and ignorance, was assailed, in the sacred language at that, and the attack was launched in the name of science and life. For the first time the ***Haskalah***, Hebrew humanism, declared war on whatever in the past trammelled the modern evolution of Judaism. In vain the Meassefim, save the exceptional few, refrained scrupulously from violent declamation against primary dogmatic principles. In vain their master Mendelssohn, contravening good sense and historical Judaism, went so far as to proclaim these principles sacrosanct. The secularization of Jewish literature and Jewish life had made a breach in the ghetto wall. Thereafter nothing could oppose the march of new ideas. The Rabbis of the period saw it clearly; hence the stubbornness of their opposition.

Beginning with this time a new class appeared among the Jews of the ghetto, the class of the ***Maskilim***, or men of lay learning and letters, a class with which the Rabbis have since had to reckon, with which, indeed, they have had to share their authority over the people.

So far as the Hebrew language is concerned, the Meassefim succeeded in purifying it and restoring it to its Biblical form. Wessely and Mendes obliterated the last vestiges of the Middle Ages, and many of the litterateurs of the period bequeathed models of the classic style to posterity. But the return to the manner of the Bible had its disadvantages. It went to extremes, and led to the creation of a pompous, affected style, the ***Melizah***, which has left indelible traces in neo-Hebrew literature. In the effort to guard the Biblical style against the Rabbinisms which had impaired the elegance of the Hebrew language, the purists had gone beyond the bounds of moderation. To express the most prosaic thought, the simplest ideas, they drew upon the metaphors and the elevated diction of the Bible. This rage for academic correctness is responsible for the reputation, not merited by Hebrew literature, that it lacks originality, that it is no more than a *jeu d'esprit*, a jumble of quibbling conceits.

Italian men of letters also took part in the literary movement of the end of the eighteenth century. Two of them are worthy of mention by name. The first is the poet Ephraim Luzzatto (1727-1792), whose love sonnets, written in a sprightly style, sound a lyric note. The other is Samuel Romanelli, the author of a melodrama, much admired by his contemporaries, and of a "Journey to Arabia."

In France, also, especially in Alsace, there were collaborators of the German Meassefim, the best known among them Ensheim. Besides, France harbored the only poet of the period who can lay claim to originality, but he was not of the school of the Meassefim. Elie Half an Halevy (1760-1822), of Paris, the grandfather of Ludovic Halevy, by far surpasses the other poets of his day in poetic temperament and fertility of imagination. Unluckily, we do not possess all the poems written by Halevy, who, moreover, was not a very prolific author. In what has come down to us his talent is abundantly proved by the charm of his individual style and the wealth of his images. The reader feels that the breath of the Revolution has blown through his pages. His "Hymn to Peace" (**Shir ha-Shalom**), published at Paris in 1804, is the apotheosis of Napoleon, whom the poet hails as "liberty rescued" and "beautiful France", the home of liberty. This unique poem is characterized by unbounded love for France and the French, the beautiful country, the free, high-mettled people, bearing love of country in its heart and in its hand the avenging sword, and cherishing hatred against "tyranny on the throne, which had changed a terrestrial Paradise into a charnel house." The poet extols the dictator not only because he is a "friend of victory", but because he is at the same time and still more a "friend of science." He salutes the victorious armies. Although they bring destruction and misery in their wake, they bear before them the standard of science, civilization, and progress.

The cry of liberty wakened a loud echo in the ghettos of even the most backward countries. Hebrew literature contains a number of curious mementos, tokens of the ardent hopes which the French Revolution and the Napoleonic conquests evoked in the breast of the Jews, whose character has little enough affinity with the rule of despotism. In numerous Hebrew hymns and songs they welcomed the armies of Napoleon as of the savior Messiah. [To name but a few among the many: an ode by the celebrated Rabbi Jacob Meir in Alsace, an ancestor of the family of

The Renascence of Hebrew Literature (1743-1885)

the Grand-Rabbin Zadoc Kahn; another ode composed at Vienna by the Polish grammarian Ben-Zeeb; and the hymns sung in the synagogue at Frankfort (1807), at Hamburg (1811), etc. The Revolutionary Code published at Amsterdam in 1795 is also worthy of mention.] Before the first flush of joy died away, the reaction set in, and their hopes were blighted. The Jews relapsed into their olden social misery. Nevertheless, the clash between received notions and the new conceptions had contributed not a little to produce a ferment of ideas and create new tendencies in the ghetto, at last aroused from its millennial slumber.

CHAPTER III
IN POLAND AND AUSTRIA
THE GALICIAN SCHOOL

The Polish scholars domiciled in Germany entered, as we have seen, into the work of the Meassefim. Presently it will appear that the movement itself was transferred to Poland, where it produced a much more lasting effect than elsewhere.

In the West of Europe Hebrew was destined to vanish little by little, and make room for the languages of the various countries. In the Slavic East, on the other hand, the neo-Hebrew gained and spread until it was the predominating language used by writers. By and by a profane literature grew up in it, which extends to our day without a break.

From the sixteenth century on, the Jewry of Poland, isolated in destiny and in political constitution, comprised the greater part of the Jewish people. The agglomerations of Jews in Poland, originating in many different countries, and fused into one mass, enjoyed a large measure of autonomy. Their fortunes were governed and their life regulated by a political and religious organization administered by the Rabbis and the representatives of the ***Kahal***, the "community." This organization formed a sort of theocratic state known as "The Synod of the Four Countries" (Poland, Little Poland, Little Russia, and, later, Lithuania, with its autonomous synod). Constituting almost the whole of the Third Estate of a country three times the size of France, the Jews were not only merchants, but also, and more particularly, artisans, workingmen, and even farmers. They were a people apart, distinct from the others. The restricted ghettos and small communities of the Occident widened out, in Poland, into provinces with cities and towns peopled by Jews. The Thirty

Years' War, which had cast a large number of German Jews into Poland, produced the effect of giving a definite constitution to this social organism. The new-comers quickly attained to controlling influence in the Jewish communities, and succeeded in foisting their German idiom upon the older settlers. One of their distinguishing traits was that they pushed the study of the Law to the utmost. The Talmud schools in Poland and the Polish Rabbis soon acquired a reputation unassailed in the whole of the Diaspora. Despised and maltreated by the Polish magnates, condemned, by reason of a never-ceasing stream of immigration and the meagre resources of the country, to a bitter struggle for existence, the Jews of Poland centred all their ambition in the study of the Law, and consoled themselves with the Messianic hope. Empty casuistry and dry dogmatism sufficed for the intellectual needs of the most enlightened. A piety without limit, the rigorous and minute observance of Rabbinical prescriptions, and a cult compounded of traditional and superstitious practices accumulated during many centuries, filled the void left in their minds by the wretched life of the masses. To satisfy the cravings of the heart, they had the homilies of the **Maggidim** ("preachers"), a sort of popular instruction based on sacred texts, tricked out with Talmudic narratives, mystic allusions, and a variety of superstitions.

By the dreadful insurrection of the Cossacks in the Ukraine, half a million of Jews lost their lives. The terror that followed the uprising during the latter part of the seventeenth and the first half of the eighteenth century threw the Jewish population of the southern provinces into sad confusion. At that moment the **Hasidim** [1] with their Oriental fatalism, and their worship of the **Zaddik** ("Saint"), whom they revered as a wonder-worker, appeared upon the scene and won the Jews of a large part of Poland to their standard. Then there ensued a period of moral and intellectual degradation, which coincided precisely with the epoch in which the civilizing influence of the Meassefim was uppermost in Germany. [Footnote 1: Literally, the "pious." A sect founded in Wolhynia in the second half of the eighteenth century, the adherents of which, though they remained faithful to the Rabbinic law, placed piety, mystic exaltation, and a worship of holy men in opposition to the study of the Talmud and the dogmatism of the Rabbis.]

The reforms of Emperor Joseph II planned for the Jews in the part of Poland annexed by Austria, especially the extension of compulsory military service to them, were looked upon by the ignorant masses as a dire misfortune. They rebelled against every change, and placed no belief in the promises made by the authorities to better their condition. They were terrorized by the severity of the measures taken against them, and, impotent to carry on a struggle against authority, they threw themselves into the arms of Hasidism, which preached the merging of self in a mystic solidarity. This meant the cessation of all growth, social as well as religious. Superstition established itself as sovereign mistress, and the end was the utter degeneration of the Austrian-Polish section of Jews.

In order to guard against the danger with which the spread of the new sect was fraught, and enlighten at least the more intelligent of the people, the intellectual Jews of Poland took up the work of the Meassefim, and constituted themselves the champions of the **Haskalah**, the liberal movement. They became thus the lieutenants of the Austrian government. By and by their activity assumed importance, and in time modern schools were established and literary circles were formed in the greater part of the villages of Galicia.

Even into Russian Poland the campaign against obscurantism was carried, by men like Tobias Feder and David Samoscz; the former the author of an incisive pamphlet against Hasidism, as well as numerous philological and poetical publications; the latter a prolific writer, the author of a collection of poems entitled ***Resise ha-Melizah*** ("Drops of Poetry", 1798).

The movement was aided and abetted by rich and influential Jews. Joseph Perl, the founder of a modern school and several other educational institutions, is a typical representative of these friends and patrons of progress. [Perl was the author of a parody on Hasidism, published anonymously under the title ***Megalle Temirin*** ("The Revealer of Mysteries"). A monograph upon parodies, a literary form widely cultivated in Hebrew, which was long a desideratum has recently been written by Dr. Israel Davidson ("Parody in Jewish Literature", New York, Columbia University Press, 1908). The Hebrew parody is distinguished particularly for its adaptation of the Talmudic language to modern customs and questions. It was made the vehicle of polemics and of ridicule, as in the case of Perl's pamphlet, or of satire on social conditions, as in the "Treatise of Commercial Men", which appeared at Warsaw, and the "Treatise America", published at New York, etc. Frequently it was meant merely to divert and amuse, as, for instance, **Hakundus**, Wilna, 1827, and numerous editions of the "Treatise Purim."]

Ha-Meassef was succeeded by a progeny of periodical literature, scientific and literary. After the ***Bikkure ha-'Ittim*** ("The First Fruits of the Times"), edited by Shalom Hacohen, Vienna, 1820-1831, came the ***Kerem Hemed*** ("The Delicious Vineyard"), edited by Goldenberg, at Tarnopol, 1833-1842; the ***Ozar Nehmad*** ("The Delightful Treasure"), edited by Blumenfeld; ***He-Haluz*** ("The Pioneer"), founded in 1853 by Erter, together with Schorr, the witty writer and bold reformer; ***Kokebe Yizhak*** ("The Stars of Isaac"), edited by I. Stern, at Vienna, 1850-1863; ***Bikkure ha-Shanah*** ("The First Fruits of the Year", 1844); ***Peri To'elet*** ("Successful Labor", 1821- 1825); "Jerusalem", 1845; "Zion", 1842; ***Ha-Zefirah*** ("The Morningstar"), 1824; ***Yeshurun***. 1847, etc. These collections of essays are of a much more serious character than ever ***Ha-Meassef*** attained to. As a rule they display more originality and more scientific depth.

To attract the intelligent among the Polish Jews, permeated as they were with deep knowledge of Rabbinic literature, more was needed than witty sallies and childish conceits in an affected style. The appeal had to be made to their reason, to their convictions, their constant longing for intellectual occupation. Their minds could be turned away from a most absurd mysticism only by setting a new ideal before them, calculated to engage feelings and attract hearts yearning for consolation, and left unsatisfied by the pursuit of the Law, the nourishment given to all who thought and studied in the ghetto.

Two men, the most eminent of the Jewish humanists in Austrian Poland, succeeded in meeting the spiritual needs of their compatriots. The Rabbi Solomon Jehudah Rapoport, one of the founders of the Science of Judaism, the pursuit that was to replace Rabbinic scholasticism, and the philosopher Nahman Krochmal, the promoter of the idea of the "mission of the Jewish people", a substitute for the mystic, religious ideal--they were the two who transformed the literary movement inaugurated in Germany into a permanent influence.

* * * * *

Solomon Jehudah Rapoport (1790-1867), called "the father of the Science of Judaism", was born at Lemberg of a family of Rabbis. His studies were purely Rabbinic, but his alert mind grasped every opportunity of acquiring other knowledge, and in this incidental way he became familiar first with French and then with German. The influence of the philosopher Krochmal, with whom he came in close personal contact, shaped his career as a writer and a scholar. In 1814, at Lemberg, he wrote, in Hebrew, a description of the city of Paris and the Isle of Elba, to satisfy the curiosity which the events of the time had aroused in the Polish ghetto. In imitation of Mendes, whose writings exercised some influence upon him, he later published a translation of Racine's "Esther" (**Bikkure ha-'Ittim**, 1827), and of a number of Schiller's poems. But he did not stop at that. His profound study of the Jewish scholars and poets of the Middle Ages turned his mind to historical investigations. In the **Bikkure ha-'Ittim** and the **Kerem Hemed** he published a series of biographical and literary studies, in which he shows himself to be possessed of large critical sense and keen judgment. In its sobriety and precision his style has not been excelled. These studies of his gave new direction to the eager minds of the age. As a result, Jost, Zunz, and Samuel David Luzzatto devoted themselves to the thorough examination of the Judaism of the Middle Ages. The outcome was a new science, the Science of Judaism.

Rapoport published also a pamphlet against the Hasidim and their wonder-working Rabbis, and various articles on the necessity of promoting knowledge and civilization among the Jews. In this way he brought upon himself the hatred of the fanatics. Appointed Rabbi at Tarnopol at the instigation of Perl, the patron of Jewish science, he was forced to leave the city by the intrigues of the Hasidim. He went to Prague, to become Rabbi in that important community, and there he ended his days.

The disciple and successor of the German Meassefim, Rapoport inherited from them the conviction which characterized the Jewish **Maskil**, that science alone and modern civilization can raise the intellectual level and improve the political situation of his co-religionists. All his life he fought for the Haskalah. He loved knowledge with disinterested devotion, and not merely because it was an instrument to promote the political emancipation of the Jews. The work of assimilation set on foot in the Occident, he realized, was not applicable in the East of Europe, and would even be useless there. No vain illusions on the subject possessed him. He was very much wrought up against such religious reforms in Judaism as, he believed, would inevitably split the people into sects, and sow the seed of disunion and indifference to national institutions. This appears strikingly in his campaign against Schorr, the editor of **He-Haluz**, and Judah Mises, and especially in his pamphlet **Tokohat Megullah** ("Public Reproach"), which appeared in Frankfort in 1846. To those who faltered, having lost faith in the future of Judaism, Rapoport addresses himself in several of his writings, especially in the introduction to "Esther", holding up his own ideals before them. Love of my nation, he says in effect, is the cornerstone of my existence. This love alone has the power to confirm my faith, for the national sentiment of the Jew and his religion are closely linked with each other. And not only this national sentiment and this religion are inconceivable the one without the other, but a third factor is joined with them so intimately as to be indispensable--it is the Holy Land.

The desire to explain rationally the Jew's love for his ancient land suggested to Rapoport, long before Buckle and Lazarus, the theory of the influence of climate on the psychology of nations. In his sketch of Rabbi Hananel (**Bikkure ha-'Ittim**, 1832), he explains the psychologic traits of the Jewish people by the fact that they resided in a temperate climate and in a country situated between Asia and Africa. Thence was derived the tendency to maintain equilibrium between feeling and reason which characterizes the Jew. Under favorable conditions, and if the Roman conquest had not intervened, the Jews would have reached the highest degree of this equilibrium, and become a model nation. That is why Palestine is the political and spiritual fatherland of the Jew, the only country in which his genius can develop untrammelled; that is why Palestine is so indissolubly attached to the destinies of Israel, and is so dear to every Jewish heart. But even in the exile, "in the darkness of the Middle Ages, the Jews were the sole bearers of light and knowledge". This is what Rapoport strove to demonstrate in his works on the scholars of the Middle Ages, and in his Talmudic encyclopedia, **'Erek Millin** (Prague, 1852), which, unfortunately, was not finished.

In this fashion Rapoport, who did not hesitate to write on Bible criticism in Hebrew, the first to use the ancient language for the purpose, endeavored to reconcile the reason of a modern mind with the faith and the Messianic hope of an orthodox Rabbi.

* * * * *

It is a significant phenomenon that the Science of Judaism, the ideal meant to replace the dry study of the Law, and fill the void left in the Jewish mind by the course of recent developments, took firm hold upon the Polish Jews, the very bodyguard of Rabbinism, of which, in point of fact, it is but a modern and rational transformation.

Yet this new science, founded on the study of Israel's glorious past, and warmly welcomed by the intellectual and the cultivated in Western Europe, could not entirely satisfy the intelligent in Polish Jewry. In an environment wholly Jewish, having no reason to nurse illusive hopes of imminent assimilation with their neighbors, from whom they were divided by every possible circumstance, beginning with moral notions and ending with political fortune, the Polish Jews resigned themselves to a sort of Messianic mysticism. But the mystic's explanation of the phenomenon of the existence of Judaism also failed to satisfy their yearnings. What they sought was a warrant in reason itself justifying the permanence of Judaism and its future. The arguments set forth by Maimonides and Jehudah Halevi contained no appeal for the modern soul. A philosopher was needed, one who should solve the problem of the existence of the Jewish people and its proper sphere from the vantage- ground of authoritative knowledge. Such a philosopher arose in Galicia itself.

Nahman Krochmal (1785-1840), the originator of the idea of the "mission of the Jewish people", was born at Brody. His chief work, published posthumously through the efforts of Zunz, the **Moreh Nebuke ha- Zeman** ("The Guide of the Perplexed of Modern Times"), is the most original piece of philosophic writing in modern Hebrew. Krochmal led the sad life of the Polish-Jewish scholar--void of pleasures and filled to overflowing with privation and suffering. His whole time was consecrated to Jewish science. He led a retired life, and while he lived nothing of his was published. On account of the precarious state of his health, he never left the small town in which he was born. However, his house became the foregathering place of the votaries of Jewish science. Especially young men eager to learn came from everywhere to sit at the feet of the master. The influence which he thus exerted during his life was reinforced and perpetuated after his death by the publication of the "Guide of the Perplexed of Modern Times", in 1851, at Lemberg.

The studies contained in this work, for the most part unfinished sketches, form a curious collection. Limitations of space forbid more than a summary of its contents, and an analysis of its chief principles.

The need of finding a philosophic explanation of Divine existence forced Hegel to formulate the axiom, that reason alone constitutes the reality of things, and absolute truth is to be found in the union of the subjective and the objective--the subjective corresponding to the concrete state of every being, that is, matter, which forms his actual reason, and the objective corresponding to his abstract state, that is, the idea, which forms his absolute reason.

On this Hegelian axiom of actual reason and absolute reason, Krochmal builds up his ingenious system of the philosophy of Jewish history. He is the first Jewish scholar who views Judaism, not as a distinct and independent entity, but as a part of the whole of civilization. At the same time, while it is attached to the civilized world, it is distinguished by qualities peculiar to itself. It leads the independent existence of a national organism similar to all others, but it also aspires to an absolute, spiritual expression, consequently to universalism. The result of this double aspect is that while Jewish ***nationality*** forms the element peculiar to the Jewish people, its civilization, its intellect are ***universal***, and detach themselves from its peculiar national life. Hence it comes that Jewish culture is essentially spiritual, ideal, and tends to promote the perfection of the human kind. Krochmal in this way arrives at the following three conclusions:

1. The Jewish nation is like the phoenix, constantly arising to new life from its ashes. It comprises within itself the three elements of Hegel's triad: the idea, the object, and the intelligence. The successive resurrections of the Jewish people follow an ascendant progression, which tends toward the spiritually absolute. Starting as a political organism, it soon developed into a dogmatically religious sect, only to be transformed into a spiritual entity. Krochmal--though he does not say it explicitly--sees in religion only a passing phenomenon in the history of the Jewish people,

exactly as its political existence was but a temporary phase.

2. The Jewish people presents a double aspect to the observer. It is national in its particularism, or its concrete aspect, and universal in its spiritualism. The national genius of all other peoples of antiquity was narrowly particularistic. That is why they were submerged. Only the Jewish prophets conceived of the absolutely and universally spiritual and of moral truth, and therein lies the secret of the continued existence of the Jewish people.

3. With Hegel Krochmal admits that the resultants from the historical development of a people form the quintessence of its existence. [See chapters IX, XVI, and others; also M. Bernfeld, ***Da'at Elohim*** ("The Knowledge of God"); and M. Landau, ***Die Bibel und der Hegelianismus*** (Dissertation).] But what he does not believe is that the essential element in the existence of a people is the resultant. The process of historical evolution is in itself an adequate reason for its existence. More rational than Hegel himself, Krochmal thus avoids the contradiction which follows from the mystical definition of existence in the Hegelian system.

For the German metaphysician, existence is the interval between not being and being, that is, the period of ***becoming***. Krochmal simply eliminates this more or less materialistic notion of the ***interval***. He substitutes the moral effects produced incidentally to the course of historic action, for the idea of effects posterior to the same action, the effects called the resultants. The more or less materialistic manner in which historic action develops replaces with him the idea of the transition period, the period of becoming, as a mysterious intermediary between actual reason and absolute reason.

Proceeding from these axioms, Krochmal, at a time in which ***Volkerpsychologie*** and sociology were embryonic sciences, explains the phenomena of Jewish history as well as the phenomena of the religious and spiritual evolution of mankind, and does it with remarkable originality and profundity.

Krochmal's ideas produced an effect not to be exaggerated upon the intelligent among the Polish Jews, who had thrown off the trammels of dogmatism and mystic hope, but were in a hesitating state of mind, casting about for the reason of their very existence as Jews. His book offered them an explanation, based on modern science and yet in accord with their Jewish essence as revealed by history and therefore satisfying to their national pride.

The Renascence of Hebrew Literature (1743-1885)

Thus Krochmal opened up a way for the seekers after enlightenment in future generations. On the ideas of the master, his successors built up their conceptions of the Jewish people. Abraham Mapu, the father of the historical novel in Hebrew, drew his inspiration from the "Guide", and in our days the well-known essayist Ahad ha-'Am has seized upon certain of Krochmal's principles, notably the importance to be attached to the spiritual element in the life of the Jewish people. [R. Brainin, in his biography of Mapu, p. 64, Warsaw, 1900.]

These two leaders, Rapoport and Krochmal, stimulated a whole school of writers, whose works established the fortune of the Hebrew language in Galicia. With more or less originality, all departments of literature and science were cultivated.

Very soon, however, the times ceased to be propitious to serene thinking and investigation of the past. Hasidism, triumphant, having conquered the whole of Russian-Poland, threatened to crush all thought and reason at the very time in which the **Kulturkampf** was battering at the gates of the Polish ghetto. Rapoport, we have seen, contended with Hasidism in a witty pamphlet. After him, there appeared a satirist of great talent, who waged pitiless war with its partisans and with all the powers of darkness.

Isaac Erter, of Przemysl (1792-1841), was the friend and disciple of Krochmal. An infant prodigy, he spent all the years of his early childhood in the exclusive study of the Law. When he was thirteen years old, his father married him to a girl of eighteen, whom he had not set eyes upon before the day of their marriage. She did not live long. Erter went on with his Rabbinic studies, and married a second time. A lucky chance brought him in contact with a Maskil who led him to the study of Hebrew grammar, and he became a devotee of the Haskalah. Encouraged by Rapoport and Krochmal, with whom he had entered into relations, he published his first satire on Hasidism. It evoked considerable comment. Persecuted by the fanatics on account of it, he could not continue to follow his vocation as teacher of Hebrew. He was obliged to quit his native city, and he went to Brody, where the circle of Maskilim welcomed him with delight. Otherwise his life at Brody was full of hardships. His wife, as courageous as she was intelligent, urged him to equip himself for some serious profession. Accordingly, at the age of thirty-three, he went to Buda-Pesth to study medicine, and five years later he returned to Brody fortified with his diploma as a physician. Thereafter he occupied an independent position, and he could dare wage uncompromising warfare with obscurantism and the mystics. He published numerous articles in the periodicals of the day. After his death, they were collected by the poet Letteris in one volume bearing the title **Ha- Zofeh le-Bet Yisrael** ("The Watchman for the House of Israel").

Erter as satirist and critic of morals is a writer of the first order. For vivacity, his style, at once incisive and elegant, may be compared with that of his contemporaries Heine and Borne. He possesses not a few traits in common with these two writers. More serious and positive than Heine, he pursues a steady aim in his satires. Tears mingle with his laugh, and if he castigates, it is in order to chasten. More original and more poetic than Borne, he thinks clearly and to the point, and the effect of his thought is in no way impaired by his stilted mannerisms. Without bias or passion, and with fine irony, he rallies the Hasidim on their baneful superstitions, their worship of angels and demons. He criticises the ignorance and narrow-mindedness of the Rabbis, and scourges the shabby vanity of the communal representatives.

Animated by the desire to spread truth and culture among his co- religionists, he does not direct his attacks against the fanatics alone. He is equally bold in driving home the truth with the "moderns" of the ghetto, the "intellectuals", boastful of their diplomas, who seek their own profit, and do nothing to further the welfare of the people in general. Corresponding to the number of articles he wrote is the number of arrows shot into the very heart of the backward system imposed upon the Jews of his country. He is the first Hebrew poet who dared expose the social evils honeycombing the curious surroundings, full of contrasts and **naivete**, amid which his people lived. This he did in a series of startling descriptions. After the fashion of Cervantes, he employs ridicule to kill off the Rabbi and murder the mystic.

Erter deserves a place in the first rank of the champions of civilization among the Jews.

Galicia gave birth also to a lyric poet of some distinction. Meir Halevi Letteris (1815-1871) was a learned philologist, but his chief literary excellencies he displayed as a poet. Like Rapoport's, his maiden effort was a translation of the Biblical dramas of Racine. His workmanship was exact and beautiful. He was a productive writer, and his activity expressed itself in every sort of literary form. He left upward of thirty volumes in prose and verse. [His poetry was collected in one volume, and published at Vienna, under the title **Tofes Kinnor we-'Ugab** ("Master of the Lyre and the Cithern").] His Hebrew version of *Faust*, published at Vienna, is a masterpiece in point of style, and it gained him conspicuous renown. He ventured upon a bold departure from Goethe's work. Desiring to transfer the dramatic action to soil wholly Jewish, he substituted for Faust a Gnostic Rabbi of the Talmud, Elisha ben Abuyah, surnamed *Aher* ("Another"). This change necessitated a number of others, which were far from being advantageous to the Hebrew version.

The prose of Letteris is heavy. It lacks grace and naturalness, qualities possessed by the greater number of his contemporaries in Russia. It should, however, be set down to his credit that, unlike many others, he never showed any inclination to sacrifice clearness of thought to elegance of style.

By way of compensation, his poetry, from the point of view of style and versification, is raised beyond adverse criticism. It merits the description classic. His numerous translations from modern poets prove the facility with which the ancient language can be handled by a master. But, having acknowledged the superiority of his style, the literary critic has said all there is to be said in praise of his work. The breath of poesy, the tone of personal inspiration, the gift of fancy, are on the whole lacking. His most original poems are nothing more than an echo of the romantic school.

Nevertheless, there is a certain simple charm diffused through some of his verses, especially those in which he pours out his sorrowful Jewish heart. His Zionist poems are perfect expressions of the national spirit. One of them, the very best his muse has produced, has been almost universally accepted as the national hymn. It Is called *Yonah Homiah* ("The Plaintive Dove"). The dove is the symbol for Israel used by the prophetical writers of the Bible. Her mournful cooing voices the grief of the Jewish people driven forth from its native land and forsaken by its God.

"'Alas for my affliction! I must roam about abandoned since I
left the shelter in the cleft of my rock. Around me rages the
storm, alone and forsaken I fly to the forest to seek safety in
its thickets. My Friend has abandoned me! His anger was kindled,
because faithless to Him I permitted the stranger to seduce me,
and now my enemies harry me without respite. Since my Friend
deserted me, my eyes have been overflowing with tears. Without

Thee, O my Glory, what care I for life? Better to dwell in the shadow of death than wander o'er the wide world. For the oppressed death is as a brother in adversity.

"'Yonder two birds are billing and cooing, and tasting of the sweets of love. They live at ease ensconced in the branches of the trees, nestling amid green olive vines and garlands of flowers. I, only I, am exiled! Where shall I find a refuge? My rock-shelter is hedged about with prickly thorns and thistles.... E'en the wild birds of prey mate happily, only I, poor mourning dove, alone among all beings alive, dwell apart. E'en those who gorge themselves with innocent blood live tranquil in their home eyries. Alas! only the righteous must weep, only the poor are stripped of all hope!...

"'Return, then, my Life, my Breath! Return, my Comforter! Hear my bitter wail of woe, lead me back to my home. Have pity on my loneliness! Restore Thy love to me, bring me once again to the cleft of my rock, and let me hide myself in the shadow of Thy wings.'

"Such moaning and dull wailing, my ear caught in the night, when the fields and the woods were bathed in Divine peace; and hearing the plaintive voice of the mourning dove, my soul knew it to be the voice of the bitter woe of the daughter of my people!"

Other writers and translators in large numbers added to the lustre of Galicia as a centre of Hebrew literature. The most important among them is Samson Bloch, the author of a geography of the world, including a sentimental description of Palestine, written in oratorical style. Joseph Efrati (1820) wrote an historical drama, **Meluhat Shaul** ("The Royalty of Saul"), which deserves mention for its fine conception. And Judah Mises, in his two works, **Tekunat ha-Rabbanim** ("Characterization of the Rabbis"), and **Kinat ha-Emet** ("The Zeal for Truth"), opposed Rabbinic tradition and the authorities of the Middle Ages. His antiquated rationalism called forth the severe reproaches of Rapoport. Nevertheless he stirred up a grave controversy, which gave rise to a series of consequences extending down to the literary warfare begun by the collection ***Ha-Roeh u-Mebakker*** ("The Seer and the Searcher"), published by Bodek and Fischmann, in which the works of Zunz, S. D. Luzzatto, and Jost are criticised.

At this point ceases the dominance of the litterateurs of Austrian Poland. The centre of literary activity was thereafter transferred to Russia permanently. Hasidism was about to take complete possession of Galicia, and Hebrew literature, confined to a few small circles, was never again to reach there the heights which it had occupied in the days of Rapoport and Krochmal.

Though the centre of the Hebrew literary movement during the earlier half of the nineteenth century lay in Galicia, yet the Jews elsewhere had a share in it. In almost all the Slav countries as well as in the Occident, in Germany, in Holland, and especially in Italy, Hebrew was cultivated both by scholars and literary men. Some of the works of Zunz, Geiger, Jellinek, and Frankel, for instance, were published in Hebrew.

At Amsterdam, out of a whole school of litterateurs, but one name can be selected for special mention, that of the poet and scholar Samuel Mulder (1789-1862). Besides being active as the editor of several collections of essays, and writing remarkable historical studies, he was the composer of poems very much admired by his contemporaries. Most of them appeared in the ***Bikkure To'elet*** ("Useful First Fruits"), which he published at Amsterdam, in 1820, under the auspices of the Maskilim society ***To'elet***. The Talmudic narrative about the seduction of the celebrated wife of Rabbi Meir, forms the subject of an excellent poem, entitled "Beruriah", on the fickleness of women.

In Germany it was chiefly the discussion evoked by the movement for religious reforms (1840-1860) that created a literature in Hebrew. To cite an instance, there was the fiery pamphlet ***Or Nogah*** ("The Bright Light"), by E. Lieberman, a masterpiece in point of style and as a satire upon the orthodox party, together with the replies of the Rabbis and the men of letters. It is curious to read pleas, in Hebrew, for the abolition of the Hebrew language, and against the maintenance of Jewish nationality. Abraham Geiger sided with the extreme reformers, while Frankel and

Zunz insisted upon the necessity of retaining Hebrew as the language of worship. Another remarkable pamphlet directed against religious reforms in Judaism must be singled out for mention, that written by Meir Israel Bresselau, entitled ***Hereb Nokemet Nekam Berit*** ("The Avenging Sword of the Covenant").

Moses Mendelsohn, of Hamburg, a German Harizi both in the character of his work and by reason of his position as a straggler of the Meassefim, was a disciple and imitator of Wessely. His Makamat ***Pene Tebel*** ("The Face of the World", Amsterdam, 1870) contain literary reminiscences.

Among the contributors to the periodical literature published in Galicia, Judah Jeiteles, of Prague (1773-1838), should be mentioned as a writer of epigrams, models of their kind. [***Bene ha- Ne'urim*** ("Youth"), Prague, 1821.]

The following one is addressed to Tirzah:

"She is as beautiful as the moon, radiant as the sun; her whole
being resembles the two heavenly luminaries. The maiden lavishes
her gifts upon the whole world, and like the two orbs she rules
both day and night."

Jeiteles also carried on a sharp pamphlet war against Hasidism. [Like the Vienna and the Brody of that day, Prague also had its literary centres. Among its Hebrew men of letters was Gabriel Sudfeld, the father of the celebrated author Max Nordau, and himself the author of a drama and of an exegetical work, which appeared in 1850.]

Hungary, whose Jews had the same customs and characteristics as the Jews of Poland, gave birth to one poet of real merit. Solomon Levinsohn, of Moor (1789-1822), was brought up in orthodox surroundings, and had to contend against all sorts of obstacles, spiritual and material. He triumphed over them, and became a scholar of serious attainments and a poet of distinction. Besides his historical studies, in German, he wrote an excellent geography of Palestine, in Hebrew, under the title ***Mehkere Erez*** ("Investigations of the Land"), published at Vienna in 1819. His poetical treatise ***Melizat Yeshurun*** (a Hebrew rhetoric), also published at Vienna, in 1846, is a master work, both as a treatise on rhetoric and as poetic literature.

The introductory poem, on "Poetic Eloquence", an apotheosis of poetry and *belles lettres*, is one of the finest ever written in Hebrew. The poet displays a rich imagination, his figures of speech are clear-cut and telling, and his style is remarkable for its classic quality. An unhappy love affair terminated his days before his genius reached the period of full flowering. [Simon Bacher, the father of the scholar Wilhelm Bacher, also won a name as an eloquent poet.]

* * * * *

The literary movement of the first half of the nineteenth century did not succeed in making itself felt among the masses. It failed to call forth a national literature of even a slight degree of originality. The Maskilim of Galicia fell into the same mistake as their predecessors in Germany. In constituting themselves the champions of humanism in Poland, in a community thoroughly religious, and affected by modern conceptions only superficially, they should not have attached the undue importance they did to arguments addressed to reason. Their appeal should have been directed to the feelings of their co-religionists. They labored under the delusion that positive reasoning could carry conviction to a people immersed in mystical speculation, crushed by the double yoke of ceremonialism and an inferior social position, and sustained only by the Messianic hope of a glorious future. If Galician humanism never spread beyond the small circles of the literary, it was only what might have been expected. It could not become a popular movement. Neither the depth of thinkers like Rapoport and Krochmal, nor the biting satire of an Erter, nor the Zionistic lyricism of a Letteris, had force enough to cry a halt to the Hasidim and impede their dark work. In point of fact, the newer ideas all but failed to make an impression on the most independent of the young Rabbis. They were affrighted by the religious decadence in evidence in Germany, and they took a rather determined stand in opposition to the spread of a secular literature in Hebrew. [Cases might be cited besides that of the learned friend of Rapoport, Jacob Samuel Bick, referred to by Bernfeld in his biography of Rapoport, p. 13. He deserted from the humanist camp, in which his Jewish feeling was left unsatisfied, and took refuge in Hasidism.] As a result, we shall see a steady decline in the position of the Hebrew litterateur in Poland, and a decrease in the number of Hebrew publications. The *Mehabber* makes his appearance as a type--the vagabond author who offers his own writings for sale, fairly forcing them on unwilling purchasers. No more eloquent index is needed to the state of a struggling literature.

* * * * *

It is questionable whether the work of the Galician Maskilim would not have been doomed to perpetual sterility, with no hope of ever making an impression on the Jewish masses, if an Italian writer had not appeared on the scene, who possessed the Jewish feeling that was lacking in his predecessors. In Samuel David Luzzatto general culture and genuine breadth of mind were united with Jewish loyalty raised to the highest pitch. He succeeded in discovering the formula by which modern culture can be brought to the religious without wounding their Jewish sensibilities. The life and work of so remarkable a personage deserve more than passing mention.

After a rather long period of inactivity in Hebrew letters in Italy, a new literary and scientific school sprang into being during the first half of the nineteenth century. It participated with notable success in the movement of the north. The celebrated critic, Isaac Samuel Reggio (1784-1854), an independent thinker, exercised enormous influence upon his contemporaries by his publications in the history of literature and his bold articles on religious reform. His chief work, "The Law and Philosophy", which appeared in Vienna in 1827, is an attempt at harmonizing the Jewish Law with science.

The best known of the poets were Joseph Almanzi (1790-1860) and Rachel Morpurgo. [The reader is referred to the anthology of the Italian poets of the period, published by Abraham Baruch Piperno, under the title **Kol Ugab** ("The Voice of the Harp", Leghorn, 1846).] Almanzi's poems were published in two collections, one entitled **Higgayon be-Kinnor** ("The Lyric Harp"), and **Nezem Zahab** ("Ornament of Gold").

Rachel Morpurgo (1790-1860), a kinswoman of the Luzzatto family, left a collection of poems on various subjects, entitled **'Ugab Rahel** ("The Harp of Rachel"), a carefully prepared edition of which was published by the scholar Vittorio Castiglioni. It is a curious document in the history of Hebrew literature. The language

The Renascence of Hebrew Literature (1743-1885)

of the poetess is essentially Biblical, her style sprightly and original, and her thought is dominated by a fine serenity of soul and unwavering faith in the Messianic future of Israel.

The following sonnet was inspired by the democratic revolution of 1848, which shook modern society to its very foundations, and in which the Jews were largely and deeply interested:

"He who bringeth low the proud, hath brought low all the kings of
the earth.... He hath sent disaster and ruin into the fortified
cities, and sated with blood their cringing defenders.

"All, both young and old, gird on the sword, greedier for prey
than the beasts of the forest; they all cry for liberty, the wise
and the boors; the fury of the battle rages like the billows of
the stormy sea....

"Not thus the servants of God, the valiant of His host. They do
battle day and night with their evil inclinations. Patiently they
bear the yoke of their Rock, and increase cometh to their
strength. My Friend is like a hart, like a sportive gazelle.

"He will sound the great trumpet to summon the Deliverer;
the righteous Sprout shall grow forth from the earth. Their Rock
will soothe their pain, He will repair every breach. The Lord
reigneth, and the earth rejoiceth aloud."

Rachel's finest poem is without a doubt the one named *'Emek 'Akor* ("The Dark Valley") in which she affirms her steadfast faith in the truths and consolations of religion:

"O dark valley, covered with night and mist, how long wilt thou
keep me bound with thy chains? Better to die and abide under the
shadow of the Almighty, than sit desolate in the seething

waters."

"I discern them from afar, the hills of eternity, their ever-enduring summits clothed with garlands of bloom. O that I might rise on wings like the eagle, fly upward with my eyes, and raise my countenance and gaze into the heart of the sun!

"O Heaven, how beautiful are thy paths, they lead to where liberty reigneth ever. How gentle the zephyrs wafted over thy heights, who hath words to tell?"

The same mystic note struck by Rachel Morpurgo recurs in the works of other Italian writers of the time. It distinguishes them strikingly from their contemporaries in Galicia and Russia, who proclaim themselves almost without exception the followers of a relentless rationalism.

* * * * *

Unquestionably the most original of all these writers, and the one who occupied the most prominent and influential place, is Samuel David Luzzatto (1800-1865). He was born at Triest, the son of a carpenter, a poor man, but none the less educated and respected. The childhood years of Luzzatto were passed in poverty and study. He emerged a conqueror from the struggle for life and knowledge. As early as 1829 he was appointed rector of the Rabbinical Seminary at Padua. Thereafter he could devote himself without hindrance to science and the education of disciples, many of whom became celebrated.

Luzzatto's learning was vast in extent and as thorough. Besides, he possessed literary taste and modern culture. In his southern temperament, feeling had the upper hand of reason. He was an indefatigable worker, his mind was always actively alert. Versed alike in philology, archaeology, poetry, and philosophy, he was productive in each of these departments, without ever laying himself open to the charge of mediocrity. He was the creator of the Science of Judaism in the Italian language, but above all he was a Hebrew writer.

He published excellent editions of the Hebrew masters of the Middle Ages, for the first time bringing to the doors of readers, scholarly readers as well as others, the works of such poets as Jehudah Halevi (Prague, 1840). The notes in these editions of his are ingenious and scientific. His own verses and poems are wholly devoid of inspiration and fancy, but in form and style they are irreproachable. [**Kinnor Na'im** ("The Sweet Lyre"), Vienna, 1835, and others.] His prose is vigorous and precise, at the same time preserving some of the Oriental charm native to the Hebrew.

His chief distinction is that he was a romantic Jew. His patriotic heart was chilled by the attacks upon the Jewish religion and upon Jewish nationalism by the German and Galician humanists. He was hostile to rationalism, and opposed it all his life. In his sight, science, the importance of which he in no degree denied, was yet not equal in value to religious feeling. This alone, he held, is able to establish morality in a position of supremacy.

S. Bernfeld, in his sketch of Rapoport, considers it a surprising anachronism that this romanticist, this Jewish Chateaubriand, should have appeared on the scene at the very moment of the triumph of rationalism in Hebrew letters everywhere. [Warsaw and Berlin, 1899] Luzzatto was the first among Hebrew humanists to claim the right of existence not only for Jewish nationality, but also for the Jewish religion in its integrity.

> "A people in possession of a land of its own can maintain itself,
> even without a religion of its own. But the Jewish people,
> dispersed in all four corners of the earth, can maintain itself
> only by virtue, of its attachment to its faith. And if, heaven
> forbid, it should cease to believe in revelation, it must
> inevitably be assimilated with the other peoples.... The science
> of Judaism, with which some scholars are at present occupying
> themselves in Germany, cannot preserve Judaism. [1] It is not an
> object in itself to them. When all is said, Goethe and Schiller
> are more important to these gentlemen, and much dearer to them,
> than all the prophets and all the Rabbis of the Talmud. They
> pursue the Science of Judaism pretty much as others study
> Egyptology or Assyriology, or the lore of Persia. They are

inspired by a love of science, by the desire for personal renown, or, at best, by the intention to attach glory to the name of Israel, and they extol certain old works for the purpose of hastening the first redemption, that is, the political emancipation of the Jews. But this Science of Judaism has no stability. It cannot survive the emancipation of the Jews, or the death of those who studied the Torah and believed in God and Moses before they took lessons of Eichhorn and his disciples."

"The true Science of Judaism, the science which will last as long as time itself, is that which is founded on the faith; which endeavors to understand the Bible as a Divine work, and the history of a peculiar people whose lot has been peculiar; which, finally, dwells upon those moments in the various epochs of Jewish history when the innate genius of Judaism wages a conflict with the genius of humanity in general, as it lies in wait without, and how the Divine spirit of Judaism mastered the spirit of humanity throughout all the centuries. For the day on which the positions shall be reversed, and the spirit of humanity shall remain in possession of the field, that day will be the last in the life of the people of Israel."

[1: Jost, in his "History of the Jewish People", etc.]

This conception of the providential role assigned to Israel is the point at which the Italian romanticist meets Krochmal, wide apart though their starting-places are. At bottom both do but interpret the ancient notion of the Divine selection of Israel and of a "chosen people". But while Krochmal regards religion as a fleeting phase in the existence of the nation, for Luzzatto religion is an essential element in Judaism, a view not unlike Bossuet's. However, it does not lead him astray. He still tries to harmonize faith with the demands of the modern spirit. The Jewish religion is in his opinion the moral doctrine **par excellence**. Like Heine he takes the world to be dominated by two opposite forces, Hellenism and Hebraism. Justice, truth, the good, and self-abnegation, whatever appertains to these is Jewish. The beautiful, the rational, the sensuous, is Attic. Luzzatto does not hesitate to criticise the masters of the Middle Ages rather sharply, chief among them Maimonides, who attempted the impossible when he endeavored to harmonize science and faith, reason and feeling, Moses and Aristotle. These are the irreconcilable oppositions in human life.

> "Science does not make us happy; the highest morality alone is capable of conferring true happiness upon us, and spiritual peace. And this morality is to be found not with Aristotle, but only with the prophets of Israel.
>
> "The happiness of the Jewish people, the people of morality, does not depend upon its political emancipation, but upon its faith and its morality. The French and German Rabbis of the Middle Ages, simple-minded and uncultured, but pious and sincere, are preferable to the speculative minds of Spain, whose arguing and rhetoric warped their judgment."

Such ideas as these involved Luzzatto in discussions and polemics with the greater number of his friends, the German Jewish scholars, whose views were far removed from his. He defied his contemporaries, as he attacked the masters of the Middle Ages. In one of his letters he goes to the length of asserting, that while Jost and his colleagues were engaged in what they believed to be the useful work of defending Judaism against its enemies, they were in reality doing it more harm than these same enemies. The latter tended to preserve the Jewish people as a nation apart, while the rationalistic criticism of the former, directed against the Jewish religion, burst the bonds that hold the nation together, and hasten its dissolution.

> "When, my dear German scholars", he cries out vehemently, "when will the Lord open your eyes? How long will you fail to understand that, carried away by the general current, you are permitting national feeling to become extinct and the language of our ancestors to fall into desuetude, and are thus preparing the way for the triumphant invasion of Atticism.... So long as you do

not teach that the Good is not that which is visible to the eyes, but that which is felt within the heart, and that the prosperity of our people is not dependent upon civil emancipation, but upon the love of a man for his neighbor, ... their hearts will not be possessed with zeal for God." [Letters, I, No. 267, p. 660.]

Luzzatto has no fondness for dry dogmatism, nor for detailed prohibitions and Rabbinic controversies. He is too modern for that, too much of a poet. What he loves is the poetry of religion. He is attracted by its moral elevation. Like Jehudah Halevi, the sentimental philosopher whose successor he is, Luzzatto feels and thinks in the peculiar fashion that distinguishes the intuitive minds among the Jews. He loves his native country, and this love appears clearly in his writings, yet, at the same time, they all, whether in prose, as in his Letters, or in verse, as in the ***Kinnor Na'im***, sound a Zionistic note.

* * * * *

Luzzatto became the founder of a school. Writers of our own day, like Vittorio Castiglioni, Eude Lolli, and others, draw upon the works of the master as a source, and they acknowledge it openly. His philological and linguistic works, the ***Bet ha-Ozar*** among others, have inestimable value, and his Letters, published by Graber in five volumes, the edition from which most of the passages cited have been taken, abundantly prove his influence on his contemporaries.

He was a master and a prophet, a gracious and brilliant exponent of the Renascence of Hebrew literature, which had been inaugurated by one of his ancestors, another Luzzatto.

A century of efforts and uninterrupted labor had wrought the resurrection of the Hebrew language. After it had been transformed into a modern tongue, in touch with all departments of thought, the sole remaining task was to make it acceptable to the masses of the orthodox Jews, and use it as an effective instrument of social and religious emancipation. This task became easy of accomplishment because Luzzatto knew how to direct the mind of his contemporaries. He found the key to the heart of the masses.

A message in verse addressed to him by a young Lithuanian poet, in 1857, gives an eloquent interpretation of the sentiment felt for the Italian *maestro* by the devotees of a budding school of literature:

"From the icy north country, where the flowers and the sun endure
but a few short moons, these halting lines speed with their
greeting away from the hoar frost, to the eloquent sage in the
southland, enthroned among the wise and extolled by the pious--to
the gentle guide whose heart burns, like the sun of his own fair
land, with love for the people whence he was hewn, and for the
tongue of the Jews." [Poems, by J. L. Gordon, St.
Petersburg, 1884, I, p. 125.]

The "icy north country" was Lithuania, in which the literary movement had just effected a triumphal entry, bringing with it the light of science, and the young poet was Judah Leon Gordon, destined to become the greatest Jewish poet of the nineteenth century.

* * * * *

Here we arrive at the end of the first part of our essay, devoted in particular to Hebrew literature in Western Europe. For its future we must look to the East.

CHAPTER IV
IN LITHUANIA
HUMANISM IN RUSSIA

We are in the Jewish country, perhaps the only Jewish country in the world. [See Slouschz, ***Massa' be-Lita*** ("Journey through Lithuania"), Jerusalem, 1899.]

The last to participate in the intellectual movement of European Judaism, the Lithuanian Jews start into view, in the second half of the seventeenth century, as a peculiar social organism, clearly marked as such from its first appearance. The Rabbis and scholars of Lithuania acquired fame without a struggle, and its Rabbinical schools quickly became the busy centres of Talmudic research.

The destinies of the Jewish population of Lithuania, so different in character from that of Poland proper, were ruled absolutely by the "Synod of the Four Countries", with Brest, and afterwards Wilna, as headquarters.

The revolutions and upheavals to which is due the social and religious decadence of the Polish Jews during the eighteenth century, barely touched this forsaken corner of the earth. Even the Cossack invasion dealt leniently with Lithuania, if the city of Wilna is excepted, and its early annexation by Russia saved the province from the anarchy and excitement which agitated Poland during its latter days.

Left to their fate, neglected by the authorities, and forming almost the whole of the urban population, the Jews of Lithuania, in the full glare of the eighteenth century, were in all essentials an autonomous community with Jewish national and theocratic features. The Talmud did service as their civil and religious code. The court of final appeal was a Rabbinical expert, supported by the central synod and the local ***Kahal***, and exercising absolute authority over the moral and material interests of those subordinated to his jurisdiction. The study of the Law was carried to the extreme of devotion. To have an illiterate, an *'Am ha-Arez*, a "rustic", in one's family, was considered a pitiable fate.

Lithuania, in fine, was the promised land of Rabbinism, in which everything favored the development of a national Jewish centre.

The natural poverty of the country, its barren soil, dense forests, and lack of populous centres of civilization, all tended to keep the Polish lords aloof. Poland offered them a more inviting sojourn. There was nothing to hinder the pious scholars who had escaped from religious persecution in the countries of Europe, especially France and Germany, from devoting themselves, with all their heart and energy, to the study of the Talmud and the ceremonials of their religion. No infusion of aliens disturbed them. The inhospitable skies, the absence of diversions, little troubled the refugees of the ghetto, for whom the Book and the dead letter were all-sufficing. They were not affected, their dignity was hardly wounded, by the haughty and arbitrary treatment which the nobleman accorded to the Jewish "factor" and steward, and by the many humiliations which were the price paid in return for the right to live, for without the protection of the lords they would not have been able to hold out against the wretched orthodox peasants. In morality and in race, however, they considered themselves the superior of the "Poriz", the Polish nobleman, with his extravagance and folly.

In the villages, the Jews had the upper hand, either as the actual owners of the estates, or as the overseers, and in the rude cities with their wooden buildings, they constituted the bulk of the merchants, the middlemen, the artisans, even the workmen. They all led a sordid life. Mere existence required a bitter struggle. Destitute of all pleasures save the intimate joys of family life, fostering no ambition except such as was connected with the study of the Law, disciplined by religious authority, and chastened by austere and rigid principles of morality, the Jewish masses had a peculiar stamp impressed upon their character by their life of subjection and misery. The mind was constantly kept alert by the dialectics of the Talmud and the ingenious efforts needed to secure one's daily bread. Even the Messianic dreams, inspired by a belief in Divine justice and in the moral and religious superiority of Israel, rather than by a mystic conception of life, gave but a faint touch of beauty and glamour to an existence so mournful, so abjectly sad.

Such was, and such in part is still, the manner in which they live--a sober, energetic, melancholy, and subtle people, the mass of the two millions of Jews who reside in Lithuania and White Russia, and send forth, to the great capitals of Europe and to the countries beyond seas, a stream of industrious immigrants, resourceful intellectually and morally.

In the second half of the eighteenth century, thanks to the peace with which Lithuania was blessed after its subjection by Russia, Rabbinical studies reached their zenith. The high schools, the *Yeshibot*, became the centres of attraction for the best of the young men. The number of writers and scholars increased considerably, and the Hebrew printing presses were kept in full blast. The ideal of every Lithuanian Jew was, if not to marry his daughter to a scholar, at least to have a *Bahur* at his table, a student of the Talmud, a prospective Rabbi. "The Torah is the best *Sehorah*" ("merchandise"), every Lithuanian mother croons at the cradle of her child.

In those days a Rabbinic authority arose like unto whom none had been known among Jews in the later centuries, and his earnest, independent genius, as well as his moral grandeur, conferred a consecration upon the peculiar spiritual tendencies prevailing in Lithuanian Judaism, which he personified at its loftiest. Elijah of Wilna, surnamed "the Gaon", "his Excellency", succeeded in resisting the assaults of Hasidism, which threatened to overwhelm, if not the learned among them, certainly the Lithuanian masses. To parry the dangers of mysticism, which exercised so powerful an attraction that the dry and subtle casuistry of Rabbinic learning could not damp its ardor, he broke with scholastic methods, and took up a comparatively rational interpretation of texts and the laws. He went to the extreme of asserting the value of profane and practical knowledge, the pursuit of which could not but bring advantage to the study of the Law--a position unheard of at his day, and excusable only in so popular a man as he was. He himself wrote a treatise on mathematics, and philologic research was a favorite occupation with him. His pupils followed his example; they translated several scientific works into Hebrew, and founded schools and centres of puritanism, not only in Lithuania, but also as far away as Palestine. From this time on the *Yeshibah* of Wolosin became the chief seat of traditional Talmud study and Rabbinic rationalism.

One of the contemporaries of "the Gaon" was the physician Judah Hurwitz, of Wilna, who opposed Hasidism in his pamphlet *Megillat Sedarim* ("A Book of Essays"), and in his ethical work ***Ammude Bet-Yehudah*** ("The Pillars of the House of Judah ", Prague, 1793), he pleads the cause of internationalism and the equality of men and races!

It would be rash to suppose that an echo of the studies of the Encyclopedists had reached a province double-barred and double-locked by politics and religion. The European languages were unknown in the Lithuanian Jewries of the Gaon's day, and his pupils sought their mental pabulum in the writings of the Jewish scholars of the Middle Ages, Maimonides, and Albo, and their compeers. The result was an odd, whimsical science. False, antiquated notions and theories were introduced through the medium of the Hebrew, and they attained no slight vogue. At the end of the eighteenth century, a certain Elias, a Rabbi, also of Wilna, undertook to gather all the facts of science into one collection. He compiled a curious encyclopedia, the ***Sefer ha- Berit*** ("The Book of the Covenant"). By the side of geographic details of the most fantastic sort, he set down chemical discoveries and physical laws in the form of magical formulas. This book, by no means the only one of its kind, was reprinted many a time, and in our own day it still affords delight to orthodox readers.

A long time passed before the Russian government took note of the intellectual condition of its Jewish subjects, who, in turn, asked nothing better than to be left undisturbed. Nevertheless, the treatment accorded them by the government was not calculated to inspire them with great confidence in it. As for a Russification of the Jewish masses, there could be no question of that, at a time when Russian civilization and language were themselves in an embryonic state.

It was only when the first Alexander came to the throne that the reforms planned by the government began to make an impression upon the distant ghetto. A special commission was instituted for the purpose of studying the conditions under which the Jews were living, and how to ameliorate them materially and intellectually. The first close contact between Jews and Russians took place in the little town of Shklow, inhabited almost entirely by Jews. It was an important station on the route from the capital to Western Europe, and the Jews were afforded an opportunity of entering into relations with men of mark, both Russians and strangers, who passed through on their way to St. Petersburg. [As early as 1780 a Hebrew ode was published on the occasion of Empress Catherine II's passing through Shklow. A printing press was set up there about 1777, and it was at Shklow that a litterateur, N. H. Schulmann, made the first attempt to found a weekly political journal in Hebrew, announcing it in his edition of the ***Zeker Rab***.] A circle of literary men under the influence of the Meassefim was founded there, and a curious literary document issued thence testifies to the hopes aroused by the reform projects planned in the reign of Alexander I for the improvement of the condition of the Jews. It is a pamphlet bearing the title ***Kol Shaw'at Bat-Yehudah***, or ***Sinat ha-Dat*** ("The Loud Voice of the Daughter of Judah", or "Religious Hatred"), and published, in Shklow in 1803, in Hebrew and Russian. The author, whose name was Lob Nevakhovich, protests energetically, in behalf of truth and humanity, against the contemptuous treatment accorded the Jews. [Grandfather of the well-known scholar E. Metchnikoff, of the Pasteur Institute.]

> "Ah, ye Christians, men of the newer faith, who vaunt your mercy and lovingkindness! Exercise your mercy upon us, turn your loving hearts toward us. Why do you scorn the Jew? If he forsakes his faith, how doth it profit you? Have you not heard the voice of Moses Mendelssohn, the celebrated writer of our people, who asked your co-religionists, 'Of what avail that you should continue to attach men lacking faith and religion to yourselves'? Can you not understand that the Jew, too, loves righteousness and justice like unto yourselves? Why do you constantly scrutinize the ***man*** to find the ***Jew*** in him? Seek but the man in the Jew, and you will surely find him!"

Like so many that have followed, this first appeal awakened no answering echo in Russian hearts. A century has passed since then, and Russia still fails to find the man in the unconverted Jew!

The hopes aroused in the Jews of Lithuania by the Napoleonic wars were disappointed. An iron hand held them down, and they continued to vegetate miserably in their gloomy, abandoned corner.

The Renascence of Hebrew Literature (1743-1885)

* * * * *

The story goes that when Napoleon at the head of the **grande armee** entered Wilna, the exclamation was forced from him, "Why, this is the Jerusalem of Lithuania!" Whether the story is true or not, it is a fact that no other city was more deserving of the epithet. The residence of the Gaon was a Jewish metropolis as early as the eighteenth century, and during the whole of the nineteenth century Wilna was the Jewish city **par excellence**, a distinction to which it was helped by several facts--by the systematic and intentional elimination of the Polish element, especially since the insurrection of 1831, by the prohibition of the Polish language, the closing of the university, and the absence of a Lithuanian population. The dethroned capital of a people betrayed by its nobility became, after its abandonment by the native inhabitants, the centre of a Jewry independent of its surroundings and undisturbed in its internal development. Without in the least deviating from Rabbinic traditions, its constitutional platform, Jewish society in Wilna was gradually penetrated by modern ideas.

The humanism of the German Jews, the Haskalah, met with no effective resistance in a comparatively enlightened world, prepared for it by the school of the Gaon. The Rabbinical students themselves were the first representatives of humanism in Lithuania. They became as ambitious in cultivating the Hebrew language and studying the secular sciences presented in it, as in searching out and examining the Talmud. Sprung from the people, living its life and sharing in its miseries, separated from Christian society by a barrier of prescriptions that seemed insuperable to them, the earliest of the Lithuanian litterateurs vitalized their young love for science and Hebrew letters with the disinterested devotion that characterizes the idealists of the ghetto in general.

A literary circle, known as the "Berliners", was formed in Wilna, about 1830. It was the pattern after which a large number were modelled a little later, all of them pursuing Hebrew literature with zeal and ardor.

Two writers of worth, both from Wilna, the one a poet, the other a prose writer, headed the literary procession in Lithuania.

Abraham Bar Lebensohn (Adam ha-Kohen, 1794-1880), surnamed the "father of poetry", was born at Wilna. He spent a sad childhood. Left motherless early, he was deprived of the love and the care that are the only consolations known to a child of the ghetto. At the age of three, he was sent to the ***Heder***, at seven he was a student of the Talmud, then casuistry occupied his mind, and, finally, the Kabbalah. The last had but feeble attractions for the future poet. His mental mould was determined by his thorough study of the Bible and Hebrew grammar, which was good form in Wilna as early as his day, and the works of Wessely, for whom he always professed warm admiration, had a decided influence upon his poetic bias.

In his first attempts at poetry, Lebensohn did not depart greatly from the achievements of the many Rabbinical students whose favorite pastime was to discuss the events of the day in Hebrew verse. An elegy to the memory of a Rabbi, an ode celebrating the equivocal glory of a Polish nobleman, and similar subjects, were the natural choice of the muse of the era, and the early flights of our author were not different. There was nothing in them to betray the future poet of merit. A little later he took up the study of German, but his knowledge of the language was never more than superficial. Haunted by the fame of Schiller, he devoted himself to poetry, and imitated the German poets, or tried to imitate them, for he never succeeded in grasping the true meaning of German poetry, nor in understanding erotic literature. To the Rabbinical student, with his puritanic spirit and austere manners, it was a collocation of poetic figures of speech and symbolic expressions.

His life differed in no wise from that of the poor Jews of the ghetto. Given in marriage early by his father, he suddenly found himself deep in the bitter struggle for existence, before he had known the transport of living, or youth, or the passions, or love, or the inner doubts and beliefs that contend with one another in the heart of man. Feeling for nature, aesthetic delights, were strange provinces to this son of the ghetto. A conception of art that is destitute of a moral aim would have passed his understanding and his puritanic horizon. Too much of a free- thinker to follow the Rabbinical profession, he taught Hebrew to children--an unremunerative occupation, and little respected in a society in which the most ignorant are not uninstructed, and in which, the choice of vocations being restricted, the unsuccessful and the unskilled naturally drop into teaching. Ten years of it, daily from eight in the morning until nine at night, undermined his health. He fell sick, and was compelled to give up his hap-hazard calling, to the great gain of Hebrew poetry. He went into the brokerage business, and his small leisure he devoted to his muse. Harassed by petty, sordid cares, this broker was yet a genuine idealist, though it cannot be maintained that Lebensohn was of the stuff of which dreamers are made and great poets. But in his mind, rationalistic and logical to the point of dryness, there was a secluded recess pervaded with melancholy and real feeling. The Hebrew language he cherished with ardent and exalted love. Is it not a beautiful language and admirable? Is it not the last relic saved from the shipwreck in which all the national possessions of our people were lost? And is not he, Lebensohn himself, the heir to the prophets, the poet laureate and high priest to the holy language? With what pride he unveils the state of his soul to us:

"I am seated at the table of God, and with my hand I guide His
pen; and my hand writes the language holy unto Him, the language
of His Law, the language of His people, Selah! O God, arouse,
awake my spirit, for is it not Thy holy language wherein I sing
unto Thee?" [**Shire Sefat Kodesh**, II, i.]

A creature of his surroundings, and a disciple of the Rabbis, as he was, the dialectics of a logician were in him joined to native simplicity of spirit, yet he never reached the point of understanding the inner world of struggles and passions that agitate the individual lives of men. For a love song or a poem in praise of nature, he thought it necessary only to copy the German authors and link together a series of pointed verses. The poem "David and Bath-sheba" is a failure. His descriptions of nature are dry and artificial. He was never able to account for what was happening under his eyes and around him. Events produced an effect upon him out of all proportion to their importance. The military and civic reforms of Nicholas I, he celebrated in an ode, in which he applied the enthusiastic praise "Henceforth Israel will see only good!" to regulations that were wholly prejudicial to Jewish interests. When some Jewish banker or other was appointed consul-general in the Orient, he welcomed the occurrence in dithyrambic verses, dedicated to the poor fellow in the name of the Jews of Lithuania and White Russia. But whenever the heart of our poet beats in unison with the sentiments of his Jewish brethren, whenever he surrenders himself to the sadness, the peculiar melancholy, that pervades Jewish relations, then he attains to moral heights and lyric vigor unsurpassed. In his three volumes of poetry, by the side of numerous worthless pieces, we meet many gems of style and thought. The distressed cry of humanity against the wretchedness under which it staggers, the sorrowful protest man makes against the lack of compassion he encounters in his fellow, his obstinate refusal to understand the implacable cruelty of nature when she snatches his dearest from him, and his impotence in the presence of death--these are the subjects that have inspired Lebensohn's best efforts. He insists constantly, Is not pity the daughter of heaven? Do we not find her among beasts even, and among reptiles? Man alone is a stranger to her, and he makes himself the tyrant of his neighbor.

But it is not man alone who refuses to know this daughter of heaven, Nature denies pity, too, and shows herself relentless:

> "O world! House of mourning, valley of weeping! Thy rivers are tears, and thy soil ashes. Upon thy surface thou bearest men that mourn, and in thy bowels the corpses of the dead.... From out of the mountains covered with snow and ice comes forth a chariot with none to guide. Within sits man and the wife of his bosom, beautiful as a flower, and at their knees play sweet children. Alas! a caravan of the dead simulating life! They journey on, and they go astray, and perish on the icy fields."

Distress round about, and all hopes collapsed, death hovers apart, yet near, remorseless, threatening, and in the end victorious.

In another poem, entitled "The Weeping Woman", his subject is pity again. He cries out:

> "Thy enemy [cruelty] is stronger than thou. If thou art a burning fire, she is a current of icy water!... Alas for thee, O pity! Where is he that will have pity upon thee?"

With a few vigorous strokes, the Hebrew poet describes the nothingness of man in the face of the vast world. The lot of the Hamlets and of the Renes is more

The Renascence of Hebrew Literature (1743-1885)

enviable than that of the "Mourner" of the ghetto. They at least taste of life before becoming a prey to melancholy and delivering themselves up to pessimism. They know the charms of living and its vexations. The disappointed son of the ghetto lays no stress on gratifications and pleasures. In the name of the supreme moral law he sets himself up for a pessimistic philosopher.

> "Our life is a breath, light as a floating bark. The grave is at the very threshold of life, it awaits us not far from the womb of our mother...."

> "Since the beginnings of the earth, we have been here, and she changes us like the grass of her soil. She stands firm, unshaken. We alone are changeable, and help there is none for us, no refuge, nor may we decline to come hither. Like an angler of fish, the world brings us up on a hook. Before it has finished devouring one generation, the next is ready for its fate. One is swallowed up, the other snatched away. Whence cometh our help?"

To this general destruction, this wildness of the elements, which the "Mourner" fails to comprehend, permeated as he is with belief in Divine justice, is superadded the malice of man.

> "And thou also, thou becomest a scourge unto thy brother! The heavenly host is joined by thy fellow-man. From the wrath of man, O man, thou wilt never escape. His jealousy of thee will last for aye, until thou art no more!"

And with all this, does life offer aught substantial, aught that is lasting?

> "Where are they, the forgotten generations? Their very name and memory have disappeared. And in the generation to come, we, too, shall be forgotten. And who escapes his lot? Not a single one of us all. None is secure from death. Wealth, wisdom, strength,

beauty, all are nothing, nothing...."
In a burst of revolt, our poet exclaims:

"If I knew that my voice with its reverberations sufficed to destroy the earth and the fulness thereof, and all the hosts of heaven, I would cry with a thundering noise: Cease! Myself I would return to nothing with the rest of mankind. Know not the living that the grave will swallow them up after a life of sadness and cruel misery? See they not that the whole of human life is like the flash that goes before the fatal thunderbolt?"

The same train of thought is not met with again until we come down to our own time, and Maupassant himself does not present it with greater vigor in *Sur l'eau*.

And the end of the matter is that "man has nothing but the consciousness of sorrow; he is naked and starved, feeble and without energy. His soul desires all that he has not, and so he longs and languishes day and night."

The uncertainty caused by the certainty of death, the terror inspired by the fatal end, the aching regrets over the parting with dear ones, these feelings, which possess even the devoutest Jew, are expressed in one of Lebensohn's most beautiful poems, "The Death Agony", and in "Knowledge and Death" the skepticism of the Maskil prevails over the optimism of the Jew.

Sometimes he permits himself to sing of the misery of his people as such. In "The Wail of the Daughter of Judah" (***Naakat Bat-Yehudah***), it would not be too much to say that there is an echo of the best of the Psalms. The weakest of his verses are, nevertheless, those in which he expresses longing for Jerusalem.

A great misfortune befell Lebensohn. The premature death of his son, the young poet Micah Joseph, the centre of many and legitimate hopes, extorted cries of distress and despair from him.

"Who, alas! hath driven my bird from my nest? Who is it that hath banished my lyre from my abode? Who hath shattered my heart, and brought me lamentation?... Who hath with one blow blasted my hopes?"

There is enough in his writings to make the fortune of a great poet, in spite of their ballast of mediocre and tiresome verses, which the reader should disregard as he goes along. Between him and his contemporary, the haughty recluse Alfred de Vigny, there is not a little resemblance. Needless to say that Lebensohn had no acquaintance whatsoever with the works of the French poet.

Lebensohn's poems, published at Wilna, in 1852, under the title "Poems in the Holy Language" (**Shire Sefat Kodesh**), were greeted with enthusiasm. The author was hailed as the "father of poetry". Besides, he published several works treating of grammar and exegesis.

When the celebrated philanthropist Montefiore went to Russia, in 1848, to induce the Czar's government to ameliorate the civil condition of the Jews and grant reforms in the conduct of the schools, Lebensohn ranged himself publicly on the side of the reformers. According to him, the degradation of the Jews was due to three main causes:

1. Absence of Haskalah, that is, a rational education, founded upon instruction in the language of the land, the ordinary branches of knowledge, and a handicraft.

2. The ignorance of the Rabbis and preachers on all subjects outside of religion.

3. Indulgence in luxuries, especially of the table and of dress.

If the first two causes are more or less just, the third displays a ludicrously naive conception of life. Lebensohn was speaking of a famished people, the majority of whom ate meat only once a week, on the Sabbath, and he reproaches them with gastronomic excesses and extravagance in dress. We shall see that his simple outlook was shared by most of the Russian Maskilim.

In 1867, at the time when the struggle for the emancipation of the Jews and internal reforms in general was at its highest point, Lebensohn published his drama "Truth and Faith" (**Emet we-Emunah**, Wilna), which he had written all of twenty years earlier. It is a purely didactic work, blameless of any trace of poetic ardor. It must be conceded that the style is clear and fluent, and the ethical problem is stated with precision. But it lacks every attempt at analysis of character, and is destitute of all psychologic motivation. These being of the very essence of dramatic composition, his drama reduces itself to a moral treatise, wearisome at once and worthless. The plan is simple enough. Sheker (Falsehood) seeks to seduce and win over Hamon (the Crowd). He offers to give him his daughter Emunah (Faith) in marriage, but she is wooed by two lovers, Emet (Truth) and Sekel (Reason).

The influence of Moses Hayyim Luzzatto is direct and manifest. Like the older author, Lebensohn, skeptic though he is, does not go to the length of casting doubt upon faith. He rises up against falsehood, hypocrisy, and mock piety, the piety that persecutes others, and steeps its votaries in ignorance. "Pure reason is not opposed to a pure religion", was the device adopted by the Wilna school.

Belief in God being set aside as a basic principle, the reason invoked by the dramatist is positive reason, the reason of science, of justice, of rational logic. In verbose monologues, he combats the superstitions and fanaticism of the orthodox. The whole force of the Maskil's hatred against obscurantism is expressed through the character named Zibeon, Jewish hypocrite and chief adjutant in the camp of Sheker (Falsehood). This Jewish Tartufe is very different in his complexity from the character created by Moliere. Zibeon is a wonderworking Rabbi, a subtle sophist, a crafty dialectician. The waves of the Talmud, the casuistry of more than a millennium of scholasticism, have left their traces in his mind and personality. In his hatred of the adversaries of the Haskalah, Lebensohn depicts him, besides, as a hypocrite, a lover of the good things of this world, and given to lewdness, which are not the usual traits of these Rabbis. The alleged Tartufe of the ghetto cannot be called a hypocrite. He is a believer, and hence sincere. What leads him to commit the worst excesses, is his fanaticism, his blind piety.

On the other hand, the dramatist is full of admiration for Sekel (Reason), Hokmah (Knowledge), Emet (Truth), and even Emunah (Faith).

On the background of the prosiness of this work by Lebensohn, there stands out one passage of remarkable beauty, the prayer of Sekel beseeching God to liberate Emet. The triumph of Truth closes the drama.

One characteristic feature should be pointed out: Neither Regesh (Sentiment), a prominent Jewish quality, nor Taawah (Passion), appears in this gallery of allegorical characters personifying the moral attributes. For Lebensohn, as for the whole school of the humanists of his time, the only thing that mattered was reason, and reason had to be shown all-sufficing to ensure the triumph of truth.

In its day Lebensohn's drama excited the wrath of the orthodox. A Rabbi with literary pretensions, Malbim (Meir Lob ben Jehiel Michael), considered it his duty to intervene, and to the accusations launched by Lebensohn he replied in another drama, called **Mashal u-Melizah** ("Allegory and Interpretation"), wherein he undertakes the defense of the orthodox against the charges of ill-disposed Maskilim.

* * * * *

If Abraham Bar Lebensohn is considered the father of poetry, his no less celebrated contemporary and compatriot, Mordecai Aaron Ginzburg, has an equally good claim to be called the foremost master of modern Hebrew prose. Ginzburg is the creator of a realistic Hebrew prose style, though he was permeated to the end with the style and the spirit of the Bible. Whenever the Biblical style can render modern thoughts only by torturing and twisting it, or by resorting to cumbersome circumlocutions, Ginzburg does not hesitate to levy contributions from Talmudic literature and even the modern languages. These linguistic additions made by him are always excellent, and in no way prejudicial to the elegance of Hebrew style. For it should be reiterated, in season and out of season, that it is a mistake to believe the neo-Hebrew to be essentially different from the language of the Bible, analogous to the difference between the modern and the classic Greek. The modern Hebrew is nothing more than an adaptation of the ancient Hebrew, conformable to the modern spirit and new ideas. The extreme innovators, who at best are few in number, cannot but confirm this statement of the case.

Ginzburg was a fertile writer; he has left us fifteen volumes, and more, on various subjects. Endowed with good common sense, and equipped with a more solid modern education than the majority of the writers of the time, he exercised a very great influence upon his readers and upon the development of Hebrew literature. His "Abiezer", a sort of autobiography, very realistic, presents a striking picture of the defective education and backward ways of the ghetto, which the critic denounces, with remarkable subtlety, in the name of civilization and progress. Besides, he published two volumes on the Napoleonic wars; one volume, under the title **Hamat Damesek** (1840), on the ritual murder accusation at Damascus; a history of Russia; a translation of the Alexandrian Philo's account of his mission to

Rome; and a treatise on style (***Debir***). He was very successful with his works, and all of them were published during his lifetime, at Wilna, Prague, and Leipsic, and have been republished since. One of his achievements is that he helped to create a public of Hebrew readers. It must be admitted that the great mass of the people were at first somewhat repelled by his realism and by his terse and accurate way of writing. Their taste was not sufficiently refined to appreciate these qualities, and their primitive sensibilities could not derive pleasure from a description of things as they actually are. This is the difficulty which the second generation of Lithuanian writers took account of, and overcame, when they introduced romanticism into Hebrew literature.

Though it was the first, Wilna was not the only centre of Hebrew literature in Russia. In the south, and quite independent of the Wilna school, literary circles were formed under the influence of the Galician writers and workers.

At Odessa, a European window opening on the Empire of the Czar, we see the first enlightened Jewish community come into existence. The educated flocked thither from all parts, especially from Galicia. Simhah Pinsker and B. Stern are the representatives of the Science of Judaism in Russia, and the contributions of the Karaite Abraham Firkovich in the same field were most valuable, while Eichenbaum, Gottlober, and others distinguished themselves as poets and writers.

Isaac Eichenbaum (1796-1861) was a graceful poet. Besides his prose writings and his remarkable treatise on the game of chess, we have a collection in verse by him, entitled ***Kol Zimrah*** ("The Voice of Song", Leipsic, 1836). His sweetness and tenderness, his elegant and clear style, often recall Heine. The following quotation is from his poem "The Four Seasons".

> "Winter has passed, the cold has fled, the ice melts under the fiery darts of the sun. A stream of melted snow sends its limpid waters flowing down the declivity of the rock. My beloved alone is unmoved, and all the fires of my love cannot melt her icy heart.

> "The hills are clothed with festive mirth, the face of the valleys smiles joyously. The cedar beams, the vine is jubilant,

and the pine tree finds a nest in the recesses of the jagged mountain. But in me sighs increase, they bring me low--my friend will not yet hearken unto me.

"All sings that lives in the woodland. The beasts of the earth rejoice, and in the branches of the trees the winged creatures warble, each to his mate. My well-beloved alone turns her steps away from me, and under the shadow of my roof I am left in solitude.

"The plants spring from the soil, the grass glitters in the splendor of the sun, and the earth is covered with verdure. Upon the meadows, the lilies and the roses bloom. Thus my hopes blossom, too, and I am filled with joyous expectation--my friend will come back and in her arms enfold me."

The acknowledged master of the humanists in southern Russia was Isaac Bar Levinsohn, of Kremenetz, in Wolhynia (1788-1860). His proper place is in a history of the emancipation of the Russian Jews, rather than in a history of literature. Levinsohn was born in the country of Hasidism. A happy chance carried him to Brody when he was very young. He attached himself there to the humanist circle, and made the acquaintance of the Galician masters. On his return to his own country, he was actuated by the desire to work for the emancipation and promote the culture of the Russian Jews.

Like Wessely, Levinsohn remained on strictly orthodox ground in his writings, and in the name of traditional religion itself he attacks superstition, and urges the obligatory study of the Hebrew language, the pursuit of the various branches of knowledge, and the learning of trades. His profound scholarship, the gentleness and sincerity of his writings, earned for him the respect of even the most orthodox. His **Bet-Yehudah** ("The House of Judah") and **Te'udah be-Yisrael** ("Testimony in Israel") are pleas in favor of modern schooling. In "Zerubbabel" he treats of questions of Hebrew philology, and with the help of documents he annihilates the legend of the ritual murder in his **Efes-Dammim** ("No Blood!"). **Ahijah ha-Shiloni** is a defense of Talmudic Judaism against its Christian detractors. Besides, Levinsohn wrote a number of other things, epigrams, articles, and essays. [We owe a new edition of all his works to Nathansohn, Warsaw, 1880-1900.]

The contemporaries of Levinsohn exaggerated the importance of the literary part of his work. Not much of it, outside of his philologic studies, deserves to be called literary, and even they often fall below the mark on account of the simplicity of his views, and especially on account of his prolixity and his awkward diction and style. Also the direct influence which he has exerted upon Jews is less considerable than once was thought. Upon Hasidism he made no impression whatsoever. In Lithuania, to be sure, his works were widely read by the Jews, but in that home of the Hebrew language the subject-matter and arguments of an author play but little part in giving vogue to what is written in the Biblical language.

By his self-abnegation and his wretched fortunes, his isolated life in a remote town, weak in body yet working for the elevation of his co- religionists, he won the admiration of his contemporaries without exception.

The fame of the solitary idealist of Kremenetz spread until it reached government circles. Levinsohn was the first of the Jewish humanists who maintained direct relations with the Russian authorities. Czar Nicholas I gave him a personal audience, and several times sought his advice on problems connected with the endeavor to ameliorate the social condition of the Jews. The founding of Jewish elementary schools, the opening of two Rabbinical seminaries, one at Wilna and one at Zhitomir, the establishment of numerous agricultural colonies, the improvements effected in the political condition of the Jews and in the censorship of Hebrew books--all these progressive measures are in great part, if not entirely, due to the influence of Levinsohn. And the educated men of his time paid the tribute of veneration to a compeer who enjoyed the esteem of the governing classes to so high a degree.

CHAPTER V
THE ROMANTIC MOVEMENT
ABRAHAM MAPU

The political reaction following upon the Polish revolution of 1831 made itself felt in Lithuania particularly. The hand of the government weighed heavy upon the people of this province. The University of Wilna was closed, and all traces of civilization were effaced.

From the arbitrariness of the Polish nobles, the Jews were rescued only to fall into the tender mercies of unscrupulous officials. As it was, since 1823 the most rigorous measures had been devised against them. They were exposed to expulsions from the villages, and their commercial and other privileges had been considerably curtailed. Besides, a new scourge was inflicted upon them, compulsory service in the army, unknown until then, a frightful service, with an active period of twenty-five years. Children were torn from their families and their faith, and the whole life of a man was swallowed up. They struggled against this new incubus with all the weapons at the disposal of a feeble population. Bribery, premature marriage, wholesale evasion, voluntary or forced substitution, were the means employed by the well-to-do to save their progeny from military service.

In order to ensure the regular recruiting of soldiers among the Jews, Czar Nicholas I, while abolishing the central synod organization, maintained the local ***Kahal*** everywhere, and made it responsible for the military conscription. The wealthy, the learned, the heads of the communities profited greatly by this official recognition of the Kahal. It enabled them to free the members of their families from enrollment in the army. In their hands, it became an instrument for the oppression and exploitation of the poor. "The devil take the hindmost!" expresses the state of mind of the Russian Jews in the middle of the nineteenth century, during the whole of the period called the ***Behalah*** ("Terror").

The reforms projected by Alexander I for the benefit of the Jews, the hopes cherished by the Lithuanian humanists, proved abortive. Reactionary tendencies made themselves felt everywhere cruelly, but chiefly they injured the Jews, forever persecuted, downtrodden, and humiliated. The profound pessimism of Lebensohn's poetry is eloquent testimony to the feelings of educated Jews. And yet, these votaries of knowledge, of civilization, the daughter of heaven, clung to their illusions. They continued to insist that only thoroughgoing reforms can solve the Jewish question. The people at large did not side with them, and even among the educated their view of the situation was not shared by the younger men. In this moral disorder, the masses of the people permitted themselves to be carried along unresistingly by the current of Hasidic views, which had long been waiting to capture the last fortress of rational Judaism. The Rabbis stood by alarmed, unable to do anything to arrest the growing encroachments of the mystic movement. Yet there was an adversary ready and equipped. In the young neo-Hebrew literature, mysticism found a foeman far more powerful than ever logic and rationalism had been.

The Hebrew language was cultivated with zeal by the educated classes, and even by the young Rabbis. It was the epoch of the ***Melizah***, and the ***Melizah*** was to supplement the jejuneness of Rabbinism and oppose the Hasidim with good results. Hebrew was in the ascendant, not only for poetry, but for general purposes as well. In the sunshine of the nineteenth century, it became the language of commerce, of jurisprudence, of friendly intercourse. Folklore itself, in the very teeth of the now despised jargon, knew no other tongue. The period produced a large quantity of popular poems, which to this day are sung by the Jews of Lithuania. The dominant note is the national plaint of the Jewish people, its dreams, and its Messianic hopes. They are essentially Zionistic.

In polished and tender Hebrew, with lofty expressions and despairful cries worthy of Byron, a poet of the people mourns the misfortunes of Zion:

> "Zion, Zion, city of our God! How awful is thy breach! Who will
> heal thee!... Every nation, every country, sees its splendor grow
> from day to day. Thou alone and thy people, ye fall from depth to

awful depth....

"Holy land, O Zion and Jerusalem! How dare the stranger trample on thy soil with haughty foot? How, O Heaven, can the son of the stranger stand upon the spot whence Thy command banishes him?" But hope is not entirely blasted:

"In the name of all thy people, in all their dwelling-places, have we sworn unto thee, O Zion, with scorching tears, that thou shalt always rest upon our hearts as a seal. Not by night and not by day shalt thou be forgotten by us."

Another popular poem, anonymous like the last, entitled "The Rose", is still more dolorous and despairful in tone. Stepped upon by every passerby, the rose supplicates incessantly, "O man, have pity on me, restore me to my home!"

Besides these and others with the same underlying ideas, the lyrics of Lebensohn and "The Mourning Dove" by Letteris constituted the repertory of the people. But soon romanticism on the part of the litterateurs began to respond to the romanticism of the masses, asserting itself as a national Jewish need.

A translation of **Les Mysteres de Paris**, published in Wilna in 1847-8, introduced the romantic movement among the Jews, and at the same time the novel into the Hebrew language. This translation, or, rather, adaptation, of Sue's work, executed in a stilted Biblical style, won great renown for its young author, Kalman Schulman of Wilna (1826-1900).

From the literary point of view, Schulman's achievement is interesting because of the kind of literature it was the first to offer to readers of Hebrew--pastime literature, fiction in place of the serious writings of the humanists. The enormous success obtained by this first work of the translator, the repeated editions which it underwent, testify to the existence of a public that craved light literature. Thenceforth, romanticism was to occupy the first place, and the **Melizah** style was appropriated for the purposes of fiction, to the delight of the friends of the Bible language.

In spite of his small originality, it happened that Kalman Schulman contributed more than any other writer to the achievement of securing a place for Hebrew in the hearts of the people. For the length of a half-century, he was regarded popularly as the master of Hebrew style. Romantic and conservative in religion, enthusiastic for whatsoever the Jewish genius produced, naive in his conception of life, he let his activity play upon all the fields of literature. He published a History of the World in ten volumes; a geography, likewise in ten volumes; four volumes of biographical and literary essays on the Jewish writers of the Middle Ages; a national romance dealing with the time of Bar Kokbah (a composite made up of a number of translations); and curious Biblical and Talmudic essays. [These works, first published at Wilna, have been republished again and again.]

His language is the Hebrew of Isaiah. The artificialities and the undue emphasis of his style, his childlike views, his romantic sentimentality in all that touches Jews and Judaism, which appealed directly to the hearts of the simple, ignorant readers who constituted his public, explain the success of this writer, well merited even though he lacked originality. His books were spread broadcast, by the millions of copies, and they fostered love of Hebrew, of science, and knowledge in general among the people. By this token, Schulman was a civilizing agent of the first rank. His work is the portal through which the Maskil had to pass, and sometimes passes to this day, on the path of development toward modern civilization.

Schulman became the head of a school. His poetic and inflated style long imposed itself upon all subjects, and hindered the natural development of Hebrew prose, inaugurated by Mordecai A. Ginzburg.

More creative writers were not long in making their appearance. Among the poets of the romantic school, a prominent place belongs to Micah Joseph Lebensohn, briefly called Mikal (1828-1852), the son of Abraham Bar Lebensohn.

Gentle and gracious in the same measure in which his father was hard and unyielding, Micah Joseph Lebensohn was the only writer of the time to enjoy the advantage of a complete modern education, and the only one of his generation to escape cruel want and the struggle for personal freedom. He knew German literature thoroughly, and he had taken a course in philosophy at Berlin, under Schelling. Along with these attainments, he was master of Hebrew as a living language. It was the vehicle for his most intimate thoughts and the subtlest shades of feeling.

His rich poetic imagination, his harmonious style, warm figures of speech, consummate lyric quality, unmarred by the blatant, crude exaggerations of his predecessors, constitute Mikal the first artist of his day in Hebrew poetry.

He made his appearance in the world of letters, in 1851, with a translation of Schiller's "Destruction of Troy", finished in style and in poetic polish. He was the first to apply the rules of modern prosody strictly to Hebrew poetry. His collection of poems, **Shire Bat- Ziyyon** ("The Songs of the Daughter of Zion"), is a masterpiece. It contains six historical poems, admirable in thought, form, and inspiration. In "Solomon and Kohelet", his most ambitious poem, he brings the youth of King Solomon before our eyes. [Wilna, 1852. German translation by J. Steinberg, Wilna, 1859.] It was the first time the love of Solomon for the Shulammite was celebrated--a sublime, exalted love sung in marvellous fashion. The joy of life trembles in all the fibres of the poet's heart.... Then, the old age of Ecclesiastes is contrasted strikingly with the youth of Solomon--the king disillusioned, skeptical, convinced of the vanity of love, beauty, and knowledge. All is dross, vanity of vanities! And the young romantic poet ends his work with the conclusion that wisdom cannot exist without faith--that faith alone is capable of giving man supreme satisfaction.

"Jael and Sisera", a noble production, treats of the silent struggle, in the heart of the valiant woman extolled by Deborah, between the duty of hospitality on the one side, and love of country on the other. The latter triumphs in the end:

"With this people I dwell, and in its land I am sheltered!

Should I not desire its prosperity and its happiness?"

"Moses on Mount Abarim" is full of admiration for the great legislator. The poet says regarding his death:

"The light of the world is obscured and dun,
Of what avail the light of the sun?"

His elegy on Jehudah Halevi is instinct with the pathos of patriotic love for the Holy Land:

"That land, where every stone is an altar to the living God, and
every rock a seat for a prophet of the supreme Lord".

Or, as he exclaims in another poem, "Land of the muses, perfection of beauty, wherein every stone is a book, every rock a graven tablet!"

Another collection of poems by Mikal, **Kinnor Bat-Ziyyon** ("The Harp of the Daughter of Zion"), published at Wilna, posthumously, contains, besides a number of pieces translated from the German, also lyric poems, in which the poet breathes forth his soul and his suffering. He loves life passionately, but he divines that he will not be granted the opportunity of enjoying it long, and, in an access of despair, he cries out: "Accursed be death, accursed also life!" His nature changes, his muse grows sad, and, like his father, he discerns only injustice and misfortune in the world. In a poem addressed to "The Stars", he fairly storms high heaven to wrest from it the secret of the worlds:

"Answer me, I pray, answer me, ye who are denizens on high! O, stop the march of the eternal laws a single instant! Alas, my heart is full of disgust over this earth. Here man is born unto pain and misery!... Here reigns religious Hatred! On her lips she bears the name of the God of mercy, and in her hands the blood-dripping sword. She prays, she throws herself upon her knees, yet without cease, and in the name of God, she slaughters her victims. This world, when the Lord created it in a fit of anger, He cast it far away from Him in wrath. Then Death threw herself upon it, scattering terror everywhere. She holds this world in her talons. Misery also precipitates herself upon it, gnashing her teeth in beast-like rage. She clutches man like a beast of prey, she torments him without reprieve...."

This posthumous collection of poems contains also love poems and Zionist lamentations, all bearing the impress of the deep melancholy and the sadness that characterized the last years of the poet's short life. A cruel malady carried him off at the age of twenty-four, and the friends of Hebrew poetry were left mourning in despair.

Romantic fiction in Hebrew, which the strait-laced life and the austerity of the educated had rendered impossible up to this time, now made its first appearance

The Renascence of Hebrew Literature (1743-1885)

in the form of translations of modern romances. They were received with acclaim by a well-disposed public greedy for novelties. The creators of original romances were not long in coming. The first master in the department, the father of Hebrew romance, was Abraham Mapu (1808-1867).

Mapu was born at Slobodka, a suburb of Kowno, a sad town inhabited almost entirely by Jews. The whole of the population vegetates there amid the most deplorable conditions, economic and sanitary. The father of Mapu was a poor, melancholy **Melammed**, a teacher of Hebrew and the Talmud, simple in his outlook upon life, yet not without a certain degree of education. He loved and cultivated knowledge as taught by the Hebrew masters of the Middle Ages. Mapu's mother was gentle and sweet. With resignation and fortitude she endured the physical suffering that hampered her all her life. His brother Mattathias, a Rabbinical student, was a man of parts.

In brief, it was misery itself, the life he knew, but the misery once surmounted, and vain desires eliminated, it was a life that tended to bind closer the ties of family love. Being a sickly child, Mapu did not begin to study the elementary branches until he was five years old, an advanced age among people whose children were usually sent to the *Heder* at four, to spend years upon years there that brought no joy to the student as he sat all day long bent over the great folios of the Talmud, except the joy that comes from success in study. Rational instruction in the Bible and in Hebrew grammar, scorned by the Talmudic dialecticians as superficial studies, was banished from the *Heder*. Happily for the future writer, his father taught him the Bible, and awakened love in his sensitive heart for the Hebrew language and for the glorious past of his people. At the same time, his Talmudic education went on admirably. At the age of twelve, he had the reputation of being a scholar, at the age of thirteen, an *'Illui*, a "phenomenon", and from that time on he was at liberty to devote himself to his studies at his own free will, without submitting himself to the discipline of a master.

Like all young Talmudists, he was soon sought after as a desirable son-in-law, and it was not long before his father affianced him to the daughter of a well-to-do burgher. At the age of seventeen, he was married. Marriage, however, did not change his life. As before, he pursued his studies, while his father-in-law provided for his wants. But soon his studies took a new direction. His pensive mind, stifled by Rabbinic scholasticism, turned to the Kabbalah. Mystical exaltation more and more took possession of him, and the day came when he all but declared himself a follower of Hasidism. It was his mother who saved him. He yielded to her prayers, and was held back from committing a perilous act of heresy.

These internal conflicts between feeling and reason, the perplexities with which his spirit wrestled, did not affect our author to an excessive degree. They produced no radical change in his personality. All his life Mapu remained the humble scholar of the ghetto, a successor of the ***Ebyonim***, of the psalmists and the prophets. Timorous, melancholy, lacking all desire for the things connected with practical life, often degraded by their own material wretchedness and by the intellectual wretchedness of their surroundings, these dreamers of the ghetto, more numerous than the outsider knows, hide a moral exaltation in the depths of their hearts, a supreme idealism, always ready to do battle, never conquered. In their persons we are offered the only explanation there is for the activity and persistence of the Messianic people.

Mapu was on the point of succumbing, like so many others, the darkness of mysticism was about to drop like a pall upon his mind, when something happened, insignificant in itself, but important through its consequences, and he was snatched out of danger. A Latin psalter fell into his hands by chance; it gave a fresh turn to his studies, and his mind took its bearings anew.

Was it curiosity, or was it desire for knowledge, that impelled him to decipher the sacred text in an unknown language at what cost soever? It is certain that no difficulty affrighted him. Word by word he translated the Latin text by dint of comparing it with the Hebrew original, and he succeeded in acquiring a large number of Latin words. He is not alone in this achievement. Solomon Maimon learned the alphabet of the German, the language in which he later wrote his best philosophic essays, from the German names of the treatises of the Talmud prefixed to an edition printed in Berlin. And many other such cases among the educated Jews of Lithuania might be cited.

These mental gymnastics, the necessity of rendering account to himself as to the precise value of each word, helped Mapu to a better understanding of the Bible text and a closer identification with its spirit.

Good fortune and material well-being are not stable possessions with people like the Russian Jews, obliged to earn their livelihood in the face of rabid competition, and exposed to the caprices of a hostile legislation. One day Mapu's father-in-law found himself ruined. The young man was obliged to interrupt his studies and accept a place as tutor in the family of a well-situated Jewish farmer.

His prolonged stay in the country exerted an excellent influence upon the impressionable soul of the young man. His close communion with nature, which quickly captivated his mind, rent asunder forever the mystic veil that had enshrouded it. Still more important was his association with the enlightened Polish curate of the village, who interested himself in the young scholar and devoted much time to his instruction. Mapu threw himself with ardor into the study of the Latin classics. He is the first instance of a Hebrew poet having had the opportunity of forming his mind upon the ample models of classic antiquity. Continuing under the tuition of the curate, he studied French, the language of his preference, then German, and, only in the last instance, Russian. The Russian language was not held in high esteem by the Maskilim of Mapu's day. In Kowno, whither he returned after some time, he was compelled to hide his new acquisitions, for fear of arousing the hatred of the fanatics and suffering injury in his profession as teacher of Hebrew.

Infatuated with the works of the romanticists, especially the novels of Eugene Sue, his favorite author, he began to think out the first part of his historical romance **Ahabat Ziyyon** ("The Love of Zion") as early as 1830. Twenty-three years were to pass before it saw the light of day. During that interval he led a life of never-ceasing privation and toil, laboring by day, dreaming by night. The Haskalah had created humanist centres in the little towns of Lithuania. In some of these, in Zhagor and in Rossieny, "the city of the educated, of the friends of their people and of the sacred tongue", Mapu finally found the opportunity to display his talents. But his material condition, bad enough to begin with, grew worse and worse. After oft-repeated applications, he received the appointment as teacher at a Jewish government school in Kowno, in 1848. This, together with the pecuniary assistance granted him by his more fortunate brother, put an end permanently to his embarrassment. Occupying an independent position, he could devote himself to his romance. Finally, the success obtained by the Hebrew translation of "The Mysteries of Paris" emboldened him to publish his "Love of Zion", and the timid author was overwhelmed, stupefied almost, when he realized the enthusiasm with which the public had greeted his first literary product.

Into the ascetic and puritanic environment in which the world of sentiment and the life of the spirit were unknown, Mapu's romance descended like a flash of lightning, rending the cloud that enveloped all hearts. A century after Rousseau, there was still a corner in Europe in which pleasure, the joy of living, the good things of this life, and nature, were considered futilities, in which love was condemned as a crime, and the passions as the ruin of the soul. Such were the surroundings amid which "The Love of Zion", a Jewish **Nouvelle Heloise**, appeared as the first plea for nature and love.

"The Love of Zion" is an historical romance. It re-tells a chapter in the life of the Jewish people at the time of the prophet Isaiah. The poet could not exercise any choice as to his subject--it was forced upon him inevitably. In order to be sure of touching a responsive chord in his people, it was necessary to carry the action twenty-five centuries back. A Jewish novel based on contemporaneous life would have been incongruous both with truth and with the spirit of the ghetto.

The time of his novel was the golden age of ancient Judea. It was the epoch of a great literary and prophetic outburst. Also it was an agitated time, presenting striking contrasts. At Jerusalem, an enlightened king was making a firm stand against the limitation of his power from within and against an almost invincible enemy from without. On the one side, society was decadent, on the other side arose the greatest moralists the world has ever seen, the prophets, the intrepid assailants of corruption. It was, finally, the period in which the noblest dreams of a better, an ideal humanity were dreamed. That is the time in which the author lets his story take place.

> In the reign of King Ahaz, two friends lived at Jerusalem. The one named Joram was an officer in the army and the owner of rich domains; the other, Jedidiah, belonged to the royal family. Joram had married two wives, Haggith and Naamah. The latter was his favorite, but at the end of many years she had borne him no children. Obliged to go forth to war against the Philistines, Joram entrusted his family to the care of his friend Jedidiah. At the moment of his departure, his wife Naamah, and also Tirzah,

the wife of Jedidiah, discovered, each, that she was with child. The two friends agreed, that if the one bore a son and the other a daughter, the two children should in time marry each other.

Things turned out according to the hopes of the fathers. The wife of Jedidiah was the first to be confined, and she gave birth to a daughter, who was named Tamar.

Joram was taken captive by the enemy, and did not return. At the same time a great misfortune overtook his family. His steward Achan permitted himself to be tempted to evil by a judge, Matthan by name, a personal enemy of Joram. He set fire to the house of his master, first having despoiled it of all there was in it. His booty he carried to the house of Matthan, and Haggith and her children perished in the flames. Achan laid the blame for the fire upon Naamah, who, he said, desired to avenge herself upon her rival Haggith. He substituted his own son Nabal for Azrikam, the son of Haggith, the only one of Joram's family, he pretended, to escape with his life. Poor Naamah, about to be delivered, was compelled to flee and take refuge with a shepherd in the neighborhood of Bethlehem. There she bore twins, a son named Amnon, and a daughter, Peninnah.

Jedidiah, shocked by the calamity that had overwhelmed the house of his friend, took the supposed Azrikam, the son of Joram, home with him, and raised him with his own children. In order to keep the spirit of his word to his friend, he considered Azrikam the future husband of his daughter, seeing that Naamah had disappeared, and was, besides, under the suspicion of being a murderess. Achan's triumph was complete. His son was to take the place of Azrikam, inherit the house of Joram, and marry the beautiful Tamar.

In the meanwhile happened the fall of the kingdom of Samaria. The Assyrians carried off the inhabitants captive, among them Hananel, the father-in-law of Jedidiah. One of the captives, the Samaritan priest Zimri, succeeded in making his escape, and he fled to Jerusalem. The name of his fellow-prisoner Hananel, which he used as a recommendation, opened the house and the trustful heart of Jedidiah to him.

Tamar and Azrikam grew up side by side in the house of Jedidiah. They differed from each other radically. Beautiful as Tamar was, and good and generous, so ugly and perverse was Azrikam. The maiden despised him with all her heart. One day Tamar, while walking in the country near Bethlehem, was attacked by a lion. A shepherd hastened to her rescue and saved her life. This shepherd was none but Amnon, the son of the unfortunate Naamah.

Teman, the brother of Tamar, by chance happened upon Peninnah, the sister of Amnon, who pretended she was an alien, and he was seized with violent love for her. Thus the son and the daughter of Jedidiah were infatuated, the one with the daughter of Naamah, the other with her son, without suspecting who they were.

Amnon, who had come to Jerusalem to celebrate the Feast of Tabernacles, was received with joy, by Jedidiah and his wife, as the savior of their daughter. He was made at home in their house, and won general favor by reason of his excellent character. The young shepherd felt attracted to the study of sacred subjects. He frequented the school of the prophets, and he was particularly entranced with the eloquence of the great Isaiah.

The pretended Azrikam did not view the friendship established between Tamar and Amnon with a favorable eye. He took the priest Zimri into his confidence, and made him his accomplice and aid in disposing of his rival. Jedidiah, meanwhile, remained faithful to his promise, and persisted in his intention of giving his daughter in marriage to Azrikam, in spite of her own wishes in the matter. When the tender feeling between Tamar and Amnon became evident, Jedidiah dismissed the latter from his house.

The period treated of is the most turbulent in the history of Judea. The conflict of passions and intrigues is going on that preceded the downfall of the kingdom of Judah and the great Assyrian invasion. Moral disorder reigns everywhere, iniquity and lies rule in place of justice. The upright tremble and hope, encouraged by the prophets. The wicked are defiant, and give themselves up shamelessly to their debauches.

"Let us drink, let us sing!" exclaimed the crowd of the impious. "Who knows whether to-morrow finds us alive!"

Zimri meditates a master stroke. Every evening Amnon betook himself to a little hut on the outskirts of the town, where his mother and his sister lived. Zimri surprises him. He takes Tamar and Teman there, and they watch Amnon embrace his sister. Now all is over. A dreadful blow is dealt the love of brother and sister, who are ignorant of the bonds of kinship uniting Amnon and Peninnah. Repulsed by Tamar, for he knows not what reason, Amnon leaves Jerusalem, despair in his heart.

All is not lost yet. Maltreated by his own son and plagued by remorse, Achan confesses his misdeeds to the alleged Azrikam, and reveals his real origin to him. Furious, Azrikam thinks of nothing but to get rid of his father. He sets his father's house afire, but, before his death, Achan makes a confession to the court. Everything is disclosed, and everything is cleared up. Tamar, now made aware of the error she has committed, is inconsolable at having separated from Amnon.

Meantime the political events take their course. The brave king Hezekiah carries on the struggle against his minister Shebnah, who desires to surrender the capital to the Assyrians. The miraculous defeat of the enemy at the gates of Jerusalem assures the triumph of Hezekiah. Peace and justice are established once more.

During this time, Amnon, taken prisoner in war and sold as slave to a master living on one of the Ionian isles, has found his father Jorara there. Both together succeed in making good their escape, and they return to Jerusalem.

The joy of the Holy City delivered from the invader coincides with the joy of the two reunited families, whose cherished wishes are realized. The loves of Tamar and Amnon, and Teman and Peninnah, triumph.

This is the frame of the novel, which recalls the wonder-tales of the eighteenth century. From the point of view of romantic intrigue, study of character, and development of plot, it is a puerile work. The interest does not reside in the romantic story. Borrowed from modern works, the fiction rather injures Mapu's novel, which is primarily a poem and an historical reconstruction. "The Love of Zion" is more than an historical romance, more than a narrative invented by an imaginative romancer--it is ancient Judea herself, the Judea of the prophets and the kings, brought to life again in the dreams of the poet. The reconstruction of Jewish society of long ago, the appreciation of the prophetic life, the local color, the majesty of the descriptions of nature, the vivid and striking figures of speech, the elevated and vigorous style, everything is so instinct with the spirit of the Bible that, without the romantic story, one would believe himself to be perusing a long-lost and now recovered book of poetry of ancient Judea.

Dreamy, guileless, ignorant of the actual and complicated phenomena of modern life, Mapu was able to identify himself with the times of the prophets so well that he confounded them with modern times. He committed the anachronism of transporting the humanist ideas of the Lithuanian Maskil to the period of Isaiah. But by reason of wishing to show himself modern, he became ancient. He was not even aware of the fact that he was restoring the past with its peculiar civilization, its manners, and ideas.

None the less his aim as a reformer was attained. Guided by prophetic intuition, Mapu accomplished a task making for morality and culture. To men given over to a degenerate asceticism, or to a mystic attitude hostile to the present, he revealed a glorious past as it really had been, not as their brains, weighed down by misery and befogged by ignorance, pictured it to have been. He showed them, not the Judea of the Rabbis, of the pious, and the ascetics, but the land blessed by nature, the land where men took joy in living, the land of life, flowing with gaiety and love, the land of the Song of Songs and of Ruth. He drew Isaiah for them, not as a saintly Rabbi or a teller of mystical dreams, but a poetic Isaiah, patriot, sublime moralist, the prophet of a free Judea, the preacher of earthly prosperity, of goodness, and justice, opposing the narrow doctrines and minute and senseless ceremonialism inculcated by the priests, who were the predecessors of the Rabbis.

The lesson of the novel is an exhortation to return to a natural life. It presents a world of pleasure, of feeling, of joyous living, justified and idealized in the name of the past. It sets forth the charms of rural life in a succession of poetic pictures. Judea, the pastoral land, passes under the eyes of the reader. The blithe humor of the vine- dressers, the light-heartedness of the shepherds, the popular festivals with their outbursts of joy and high spirits, are reproduced with masterly skill. The moral grandeur of Judea appears in the magnificent description of a whole people assembled to celebrate the Feast in the Holy City, and in the impassioned discourses of the prophets, who openly criticise the great and the priests in the name of justice and truth. But especially it is love that pervades the work, love, chaste and ingenuous, apotheosized in the relation of Amnon and Tamar.

The impression that was made by the book is inconceivable. It can be compared with nothing less than the effect produced by the publication of the *Nouvelle Heloise*.

At last the Hebrew language had found the master who could make the appeal to popular taste, who understood the art of speaking to the multitude and touching them deeply. The success of the book was impressive. In spite of the fanatical intriguers, who looked with horror upon this profanation of the holy language, the novel made its way everywhere, into the academies for Rabbinical students, into the very synagogues. The young were amazed and entranced by the poetic flights and by the sentimentalism of the book. A whole people seemed to be reborn unto life, to emerge from its millennial lethargy. Upon all minds the comparison between ancient grandeur and actually existing misery obtruded itself.

The Lithuanian woods witnessed a startling spectacle. Rabbinical students, playing truant, resorted thither to read Mapu's novel in secret. Luxuriously they lived the ancient days over again. The elevated love celebrated in the book touched all hearts, and many an artless romance was sketched in outline.

But the greatest beneficiary of the new movement ushered into being by the appearance of "The Love of Zion" was the Hebrew language, revived in all its splendor.

> "I have searched out the ancient Latin in its majestic vigor, the German with its depth of meaning, the French full of charm and ravishing expressions, the Russian in the flower of its youth. Each has qualities of its own, each is crowned with beauty. But in the face of all of them, whose voice appeals unto me? Is it not thy voice, my dove? How pellucid is thy word, though its music issues from the land of destruction!... The melody of thy words sings in my ear like a heavenly harp."

This idealization of a language of the past, and of that past itself, produced an enormous effect upon all minds, and it prepared the soil for an abundant harvest. The success won by "The Love of Zion" encouraged Mapu to publish his other historical romance, the action of which is placed in the same period as the first work. ***Ashmat Shomeron*** ("The Transgression of Samaria"), also published at Wilna, is an epic in the true sense. It reproduces the conflicts set afoot by the rivalry between Jerusalem and Samaria. The underlying idea in this novel is not unlike that of "The Love of Zion". But the author allows himself to run riot in the use of antitheses and contrasts. He arraigns the poor inhabitants of Samaria with pitiless severity. Whatever is good, just, beautiful, lofty, and chaste in love, proceeds from Jerusalem; whatever savors of hypocrisy, crookedness, dogmatism, absurdity, sensuality, proceeds from Samaria. The author is particularly implacable toward the hypocrites, and toward the blind fanatics with their narrow-mindedness. The personification of certain types of ghetto fanatics is a transparent ruse. The book excited the anger of the obscurantists, and, in their wrath, they persecuted all who read the works of Mapu.

"The Transgression of Samaria" shares a number of faults of technique with the first novel, but also it is equally with the other a product of rich imaginativeness and epic vigor. In reproducing local color and the Biblical life, the author's touch is even surer than in "The Love of Zion".

If one were inclined to apply to Mapu's novels the standards of art criticism, a radical fault would reveal itself. Mapu is not a psychologist. He does not know how to create heroes of flesh and blood. His men and women are blurred, artificial. The moral aim dominates. The plot is puerile, and the succession of events tiresome. But these shortcomings were not noticed by his simple, uncultivated readers, for the reason that they shared the artless *naivete* of the author.

Besides these two, we have some poetic fragments of a third historical romance by Mapu, which was destroyed by the Russian censor. There is also an excellent manual of the Hebrew language, **Amon Padgug** ("The Master Pedagogue"), very much valued by teachers of Hebrew, and, finally, a method of the French language In Hebrew.

We shall revert elsewhere to his last novel, '**Ayit Zabua**' ("The Hypocrite"), which is very different in style and character from his first two romances.

In his last years he was afflicted with a severe disease. Unable to work, he was supported by his brother, who had settled in Paris, and who invited Mapu to join him there. On the way, death overtook him, and he never saw the capital of the country for which he had expressed the greatest admiration all his life.

In southern Russia, especially at Odessa, literary activity continued to be carried on with success. Abraham Bar Gottlober (1811-1900), writing under the pseudonym Mahalalel, was the most productive of the poets, if not the best endowed of the whole school.

A disciple of Isaac Bar Levinsohn, and visibly affected by the influence of Wessely and Abraham Bar Lebensohn, he devoted himself to poetry. The first volume of his poems appeared at Wilna in 1851. Toward the end of his days, he published his complete works in three volumes, ***Kol Shire Mahalalel*** ("Collected Poems", Warsaw, 1890). His earliest productions go back to the middle of the last century. He is a remarkable stylist, and, in some of his works, his language is both simple and polished. "Cain", or the Vagabond, is a marvel in style and thought.

In the poem entitled "The Bird in the Cage", he writes as a Zionist, and he weeps over the trials of his people in exile. In another poem, ***Nezah Yisrael*** ("The Eternity of Israel"), perhaps the best that issued from his pen, he puts forward a dignified claim to his title as Jew, of which he is proud.

> "Judah has neither bow nor warring hosts, nor avenging dart, nor sharpened sword. But he has a suit in the name of justice with the nations that contend with him....
>
> "I take good heed not to recount to you our glory. Why should I extol the eternal people, for you detest its virtues, you desire not to hear of them.... But remember, ye peoples, if I commit a transgression, not in me lies the wrong--through your sin I have stumbled....
>
> "I ask not for pity, I ask but for justice."

On the whole, Gottlober lacks poetic warmth. In the majority of his poems, his style errs on the side of prolixity and wordiness. He has made a number of translations into Hebrew, and his prose is excellent. His satires frequently display wit. His versified history of Hebrew poetry, contained in the third volume of his works, is inferior to the ***Melizat Yeshurun*** by Solomon Levinsohn referred to above. Later he published a monthly review in Hebrew, under the title ***Ha-Boker Or*** ("The Clear Morning"). His reminiscences of the Hasidim, whom he opposed all his life, are the best of his prose writings, and put him in a class with the realists. He also wrote a history of the Kabbalah and Hasidism (***Toledot ha-Kabbalah weha-Hasidut***). [In the monthly ***Ha-Boker Or***, and ***Orot me-Ofel*** ("Gleams in the Darkness"), Warsaw, 1881.]

Gottlober was the *Mehabber* personified, the type of the vagabond author, who is obliged to go about in person and force his works upon patrons in easy circumstances.

The number of writers belonging to the romantic school, by reason of the form of their works, or by reason of their content, is too large for us to give them all by name. Only a few can be mentioned and characterized briefly.

Elias Mordecai Werbel (1805-1880) was the official poet of the literary circle at Odessa. A collection of his poems, which appeared at Odessa, is distinguished by its polished execution. Besides odes and occasional poems, they contain several historical pieces, the most remarkable of them "Huldah and Bor", Wilna, 1848, based on a Talmudic legend. [In *Keneset Yisrael*, Warsaw, 1888.]

He was excelled by Israel Roll (1830-1893), a Galician by birth, but living in Odessa. His *Shire Romi* ("Roman Poems"), all translated from the works of the great Latin poets, give evidence of considerable poetic endowment. His style is classic, copious, and precise, and his volume of poems will always maintain a place in a library of Hebrew literature by the side of Mikal's version of Ovid and the admirable translation of the Sibylline books made by the eminent philologist Joshua Steinberg.

In prose, first place belongs to Benjamin Mandelstamm (died 1886). Among his works is a history of Russia, but his most important production, *Hazon la-Mo'ed*, is a narrative of his travels and the impressions he received in the "Jewish zone", chiefly Lithuania. In certain respects, he must be classified with Mordecai A. Ginzburg, with whom he shares clarity of thought and wit. But his sentimentality, and his excessive indulgence in certain affectations of style, range him with the romantic poets.

The distinguished poet Judah Leon Gordon in his beginnings also belonged to the romantic school. His earliest poems, especially "David and Michal", treat of Bible times. But Gordon did not remain long in sympathy with the endeavors of the romanticists, and the mature stage of his literary activity belongs to a later epoch.

The characteristic trait of Hebrew romanticism, which distinguishes it from most analogous movements in Europe, is that it remained in the path of orderly progress and emancipation. It showed no sign of turning aside toward reactionary measures in religion or in other concerns. Neither the retrograde policy adopted by the government against the Jews, nor the uncompromising fanaticism of certain parties among the Jews themselves, could arrest the development of the humanitarian ideas disseminated by the Austrian and the Italian school.

Since the origin of the German Meassefim movement, the evolution of Hebrew literature has not been stopped for a single instant in its striving for knowledge and light. The romantic movement is one of its most characteristic stages, and at the same time one most productive of good results. The sombre present held out no promises for the future, and the dark clouds on the political horizon eclipsed every hope of better fortunes. At such a time the champions of the Haskalah opposed ignorance and prejudice in the name of the past, and in the name of morality and idealism they sought to win the hearts of the populace for the "Divine Haskalah".

The influence of Hebrew romanticism was many-sided. The blending of the rationalism of the first humanists with the patriotic sentiments of Luzzatto fortified the bonds that united the writers to the mass of the faithful believers. A sentimentalism that was called forth by a poetic revival of the times of the prophets did more for the diffusion of sane and natural ideas than exhortations and arguments without end, and the declaration, repeated again and again by the school of Wilna, that science and faith stand in no sort of opposition to each other, was an equally powerful means of bringing together the educated with the moderate among the religious.

Soon the times were to become more favorable to a renewal of the combat with the obscurants, and then the antagonism between the educated classes and the orthodox would be resumed with fresh vigor. When that time arrived, a whole school of ardent realistic writers set themselves the task of counteracting the misery of Jewish life, and they executed it without sparing the susceptibilities and the self-love of the religious masses. They rose up in judgment against orthodox and traditional Judaism; they chastised it and traduced it. With acerbity they promulgated the gospel of modern humanism and the surrender of outward beliefs. By their side, however, we shall see a more moderate school claim its own, and one not less efficient. It will proclaim words of charity, faith, and hope. To the negations and destructive aphorisms of the realistic school it will oppose firm confidence in the early regeneration of the Jewish people, called to fulfil its destiny upon its national soil. The Zionist appeal will unite the orthodox masses and the emancipated youth in a single transport of action and hope.

CHAPTER VI
THE EMANCIPATION MOVEMENT
THE REALISTS

The accession of Alexander II to the throne marks a decisive moment in the history of the Russian empire. The fresh impetus that proceeded from the generous and liberal ideas encouraged by the Czar himself reached the ghetto. Substantial improvements in the political situation of the Jews the empire and the easier access to the liberal professions granted them, the abolition of the old order of military service and the suppression of the Kahal--these, joined to the expectation of an early civil emancipation, stirred the Jewish humanists profoundly. Startled out of their age-long dreams, the Jews with a modern education found themselves suddenly face to face with reality, and engaged in a struggle with the exigencies of modern life. In justice to them it must be said that they realized at once where their duty lay, and they were not found wanting.

They ranged themselves on the side of the reform government, and with all their strength they tried to neutralize the resistance with which the conservative Jews met the reforms, projected or achieved. They were particularly active in the regions remote from the large cities, which had hardly been touched by the new currents. Early in the struggle, the creation of a Hebrew press placed an effective instrument in the hands of the defenders of the new order.

The interest aroused among the Jews by the Crimean War suggested the idea of a political and literary journal in Hebrew to Eliezer Lipman Silberman. It was called ***Ha-Maggid*** ("The Herald"), and the first issue appeared in 1856, in the little Prussian town of Lyck, situated on the Russo-Polish frontier. It was successful beyond expectation. The enthusiasm of the readers at sight of the periodical published in the holy language expressed itself in dithyrambic eulogies and a vast number of odes that filled its columns. The influence it exercised was great. It formed a meeting-place for the educated Jews of all countries and all shades of opinion. Besides news bearing on politics and literature, and philological essays, and poems more or less bombastic, **Ha-Maggid** published a number of original articles of great value. Its issues formed the link between the old masters, Rapoport and Luzzatto, and young Russian writers like Gordon and Lilienblum.

The learned French Orientalist Joseph Halevy, later the author of an interesting collection of Hebrew poems, used **Ha-Maggid** for the promulgation of his bold ideas on the revival of Hebrew, and its practical adjustment to modern notions and needs by means of the invention of new terms. In part, his propositions have been realized in our own days. To Rabbi Hirsch Kalisher and the editor, David Gordon, as the first promoters of the Zionist idea, **Ha-Maggid** gave the opportunity, as early as 1860, of urging its practical realization, and due to their propaganda the first society was formed for the colonization of Palestine.

This pioneer venture in the field of Hebrew journalism stimulated many others. Hebrew newspapers sprang up in all countries, varying in their tendencies according to their surroundings and the opinions of their editors. In Galicia especially, where there was no absurd censorship to manacle thought, Hebrew journals were published in abundance. In Palestine, in Austria, at one time in Paris even, periodicals were founded, and they created a public opinion as well as readers. But it was above all in Russia, in the measure in which the censorship was relaxed, that the Hebrew press became eventually a popular tribunal in the true sense of the word, with a steady army of readers at its back.

Samuel Joseph Finn, an historian and a philologist of merit, published a review at Wilna, called **Ha-Karmel** (1860-1880), which was devoted to the Science of Judaism in particular.

Hayyim Selig Slonimski, the renowned mathematician, founded his journal **Ha-Zefirah** ("The Morningstar") in 1872. It was issued first in Berlin and later in Warsaw. He himself wrote a large number of articles in it, in his chosen field as popularizer of the natural sciences.

In Galicia, Joseph Kohen-Zedek published **Ha-Mebasser** ("The Messenger") and **Ha-Nesher** ("The Eagle"), and Baruch Werber, **Ha-'Ibri** ("The Hebrew").

By far outstripping all these in importance was the first Hebrew journal that appeared in Russia, ***Ha-Meliz*** ("The Interpreter"), founded at Odessa in 1860, by Alexander Zederbaum, one of the most faithful champions of humanism. ***Ha-Meliz*** became the principal organ of the movement for emancipation, and the spokesman of the Jewish reformers.

The Hebrew press with all its shortcomings, and in spite of its meagre resources, which prevented it from securing regular, paid contributors, and left it at the mercy of an irresponsible set of amateurs, yet exercised considerable influence upon the Jews of Russia. [Sometimes ten readers clubbed together for one subscription.] Unremittingly it busied itself with the spread of civilization, knowledge, and Hebrew literature.

In the large centres, especially in the more recently established communities in the south of Russia, the intellectual emancipation of the Jews was an accomplished fact at an early day. The young people streamed to the schools, and applied themselves voluntarily to manual trades. The professional schools and the Rabbinical seminaries established by the government robbed the ***Hedarim*** and the ***Yeshibot*** of thousands of students. The Russian language, hitherto neglected, began to dispute the first place with the jargon and even the Hebrew. Wherever the breath of economic and political reforms had penetrated, emancipation made its way, and without encountering serious opposition on the part of traditional Judaism.

Wilna, the capital of Lithuania, sorely tried by the Polish insurrection of 1863, and intentionally excluded by the government from the benefits of all administrative and political reforms, did not continue to be the centre of the new life of the Russian Jews, as it had been of their old life. The "Lithuanian Jerusalem" had put aside its sceptre, and it lay down for a long sleep, with dreams of the Haskalah, "twin-sister of faith". As Wilna has since that time witnessed no excesses of fanaticism, so also it has not known an intense life, the acrid opposition between Haskalah and religion. It remained the capital of the moderate, traditional attitude and religious opportunism.

By way of compensation, the small country towns and the Talmudic centres in Lithuania put up a stubborn resistance to the new reforms. The poor literary folk stranded in out-of-the-way corners far removed from civilization were treated as pernicious heretics. Nothing could stop the fanatics in their persecution, and they had recourse to the extremest expedients. Made to believe that the reformers harbored designs against the fundamental principles of Judaism, the people, deluded and erring, thought the obscurantists right and applauded them, while they rose up against the modernizers as one man.

The opposition between humanism and the religious fanatics degenerated into a remorseless struggle. The early Haskalah, the gentle, celestial daughter of dreamers, was a thing of the past. The educated classes, conscious of the support of the authorities and of the public opinion prevailing in the centres of enlightenment, became aggressive, and made a bold attack upon the course and ways of the traditionalists. They displayed openly, with bluntest realism, all the evils that were corroding the system of their antagonists. They followed the example of the Russian realistic literature of their day, in exposing, branding, scourging, and chastising whatever is old and antiquated, whatever mutinies against the modern spirit. Such is the character of the realistic literature succeeding the epoch of the romanticists.

The signal was again given by Abraham Mapu, in his novel descriptive of the manners of the small town, '**Ayit Zabua**' ("The Hypocrite"), of which the early volumes appeared about the year 1860, at Wilna. In view of the growing insolence of the fanatics, and the urgency of the reforms projected by the government, the master of Hebrew romance decided to abandon the poetic heights to which his dreams had been soaring. He threw himself into the scrimmage, adding the weight of his authority to the efforts of those who were carrying on the combat with the obscurantists. Even in his historical romances, especially in the second of them, he had permitted his hatred against the hypocrites of the ghetto, disguised in the skin of the false prophet Zimri and his emulators, to make itself plainly visible. Now he unmasked them in full view of all, and without regard for the feelings of the other party.

"The Hypocrite" is an ambitious novel in five parts. All the types of ghetto fanatics are portrayed with the crudest realism. The most prominent figure is Rabbi Zadok, canting, unmannerly, lewd, an unscrupulous criminal, covering his malpractices with the mantle of piety. He is the prototype of all the Tartufes of the ghetto, who play upon the ignorance and credulity of the people. His chief follower, Gadiel, is a blind fanatic, an implacable persecutor of all who do not share his opinions, the enemy of Hebrew literature, embittering the life of any who venture to read a modern publication. Devoted adherent of the Haskalah as he was, Mapu was not sparing of paint in blackening these enemies of culture.

Around his central figure a large number of characters are grouped, each personifying a type peculiar to the Lithuanian province. The darkest portrait is that of Gaal, the ignorant upstart who rules the whole community, and makes common cause with Rabbi Zadok and his followers. The venality of the officials gives the heartless ***parvenu*** free scope for his arbitrary misdeeds, and without let or hindrance he persecutes all who are suspected of modernizing tendencies. He is enveloped in an atmosphere of crime and terror. Mapu was guilty of overdrawing his characters; he exceeded the limits of truth. On the other hand, he grows more indulgent and more veracious when he describes the life of the humbler denizens of the ghetto.

Jerahmeel, the **Batlan**, is a finished product. The **Batlan** is a species unknown outside of the ghetto. In a sense, he is the bohemian in Jewry. His distinguishing traits are his oddity and farcical ways. Not that he is an ignoramus--far from that. In many instances he is an erudite Talmudist, but his simplicity, his absent-mindedness, his lack of all practical sense, incapacitate him from undertaking anything, of whatever nature it may be. He is a parasite, and by reason of mere inertia he becomes attached to the enemies of progress.

The **Shadhan**, the influential matrimonial agent lacking in no Jewish community, is painted true to life. Spiteful, cunning, witty, even learned, he excels in the art of bringing together the eligibles of the two sexes and unravelling intricate situations.

The most sympathetic figure in the whole novel is the honest burgher. Mapu has given us the idealization of the large class of humble tradesmen who have been well grounded in the Talmud, who are endowed with an open heart for every generous feeling, and whose good common sense and profoundly moral character the congested condition of the ghetto has not succeeded in perverting.

All these figures represent real individuals, living and acting. Mapu has without a doubt exaggerated reality, and frequently to the detriment of truth. Nevertheless they remain veracious types.

On the other hand, he has not succeeded so well in the creation of the Maskilim type. The new generation, the enlightened friends of culture, are puppets without life, without personality, who speak and move only for the purpose of glorifying the "Divine Haskalah".

Mapu's conception of Jewish life can be summed up in two phrases: ***enlightened***, hence good, just, generous; ***fanatic***, hence wicked, hypocritical, lewd, cowardly.

If the novel on account of its treatment of the subject has some claims upon the description realistic, it has none by reason of its form. "The Hypocrite" suffers from all the defects of Mapu's historical romances, which, in the work under consideration, take on a graver aspect. The style of Isaiah and poetic flights do not comport well with a modern subject and a modern environment. Herein, again, Mapu's example became pernicious for his successors.

When the novel is in full swing, there occurs a series of letters written by one of the heroes from Palestine. The enthusiasm of the author for the Holy Land cannot deny itself, and this unexpected Zionist note, in a purely modern work, reveals his soul as it really is, the soul of a great dreamer.

It was after the appearance of Mapu's "Hypocrite", in the year 1867, that Abraham Bar Lebensohn published, at Wilna, his drama "Truth and Faith", written twenty years before, in which, also, the Tartufe of the ghetto plays a great part.

At about the same time a young writer, Solomon Jacob Abramowitsch, issued his realistic novel ***Ha-Abot weha-Banim*** ("Fathers and Sons", Zhitomir, 1868). Abramowitsch had already acquired some fame by a natural history (***Toledot ha-Teba'***) in four volumes, in which he taxed his ingenuity to create a complete nomenclature for zoology in Hebrew. His novel is a failure. The subject is the antagonism between religious fathers and emancipated sons, and the action takes place in Hasidic surroundings. There is nothing to betray the future master, the delicate satirist, the admirable painter of manners. Abramowitsch then turned away from Hebrew for a while, and made the literary fortune of the Jewish-German jargon by writing his tales of Jewish life in it, but about ten years ago he re-entered the ranks of the writers of Hebrew, and became one of the most original authors handling the sacred language. What distinguishes Abramowitsch from his contemporaries is his style. He was among the first to introduce the diction of the Talmud and the Midrash into modern Hebrew. The result is a picturesque idiom, to which the Talmudic expressions give its peculiar charm. Though it continues essentially Biblical, the new element in it puts it into perfect accord with the spirit and the environment it is called upon to depict. It lends itself marvellously well to the description of the life and manners of the Jews of Wolhynia, the province which forms the background of his novels.

All these creators of a Hebrew realism were outstripped by the poet Gordon, who expresses the whole of his agitated epoch in his own person alone.

CHAPTER VII
THE CONFLICT WITH RABBINISM
JUDAH LEON GORDON

Judah Leon Gordon (1830-1892) was born at Wilna, of well-to-do parents, who were pious and comparatively enlightened. As was customary in his day, he received a Rabbinical education, but at the same time he was not permitted to neglect the study of the Bible and the classical Hebrew. He was a brilliant student, and all circumstances pointed to his future eminence as a Talmudist. The academic address which he delivered on the occasion of his **Bar-Mizwah**, on his thirteenth birthday, proclaimed him an *'Illui*, and he was betrothed to the daughter of a rich burgher.

His father's financial ruin caused the rupture of his engagement, and, a marriage being out of the question, he was left free to continue his studies as he would. He returned to Wilna, the first centre of the Haskalah in Russia. The secular literature couched in Hebrew had penetrated to the very synagogue, if not openly, at least by the back door. In secret Gordon devoured all the modern writings that fell in his hands. It was the time of the elder Lebensohn, when he stood at the summit of his fame and influence. Very soon Gordon perceived that the study of Hebrew is not sufficient for the equipment of a man of learning and cultivation. Under the guidance of an intelligent kinsman, he studied German, Russian, French, and Latin, one of the first Hebrew writers to become thoroughly acquainted with Russian literature. He devoted much time to the study of Hebrew philology and grammar, and he was justly reputed a distinguished connoisseur of the language. Both his linguistic researches and his new linguistic formations in Hebrew are extremely valuable.

The muse visited him early, and by his first attempts at poetry he earned the good-will and favor of Lebensohn the father and the friendship of Lebensohn the son. In his youthful fervor, he offers enthusiastic admiration to the older man, and proclaims himself his disciple. But it was the younger poet, Micah Joseph, who exerted the greater influence upon him. A little drama dedicated to the memory of the poet snatched away in the prime of his years shows the depth and tenderness of Gordon's affection for him.

All this time Gordon did not cease to be a student. In 1852 he passed his final examinations, graduating him from the Rabbinical Seminary at Wilna, and he was appointed teacher at a Jewish government school at Poneviej, a small town in the Government of Kowno. Successively he was transferred from town to town in the same district. Twenty years of wrangling with fanatics and teaching of children in the most backward province of Lithuania did not arrest his literary activity. In 1872 he was called to the post of secretary to the Jewish community of St. Petersburg and secretary to the recently formed Society for the Promotion of Culture among the Jews of Russia. Thenceforward his material needs were provided for, and he held an assured, independent position. Denounced in 1879 as a political conspirator, he was thrown into prison, with the result that he suffered considerable financial loss and irreparable physical injury. His innocence was established, and, having been set free, he became one of the editors of the journal **Ha-Meliz**, the Hebrew periodical with the largest circulation at the time. But the disease he had contracted ate away his strength, and he died a victim of the Russian espionage system.

As was said, the young poet followed in the tracks of the two Lebensohns. In 1857 he published his first ambitious poem, **Ahabat David u-Michal**, the product of a naive dreamer, who swears a solemn oath to "remain the slave of the Hebrew language forever, and consecrate all his life to it". [The collected poems of Gordon appeared, in four volumes, in 1884, at St. Petersburg, and in six volumes, in 1900, at Wilna.] "David and Michal" rehearses poetically the tale of the shepherd's love for the daughter of the king. The poet carries us back to Biblical times. He tells us how the daughter of Saul is enamored of the young shepherd summoned to the royal court to dispel the king's melancholy. Jealousy springs up in the heart of Saul, and he takes umbrage at the popularity of David. Before granting him the hand of his daughter, he imposes superhuman tests upon the young suitor, which would seem to doom him to certain death. But David emerges from every trial with glory, and returns triumphant. The king is mastered by consuming jealousy, and in his anger pursues David relentlessly. David is obliged to flee, and Michal is given to his rival. The friendship of David and Jonathan is depicted in touching words. Finally David prevails, and he is anointed king over Israel. He takes Michal back unto himself, love being stronger than the sense of injury. The shame of the past is forgotten. But the poor victim is never to know the joy of bearing a child--Michal remains barren until the last, and leads a solitary existence. Old and forgotten, she passes out of life on the very day of David's death.

In this simple, pure drama, the influence of Schiller and of Micah Joseph Lebensohn is clearly seen. But real feeling for nature and real understanding of the emotion of love are lacking in Gordon. His descriptions of nature are a pale retracing of the pictures of the romanticists. Poet of the ghetto as he was, he knew neither nature at first hand, nor love, nor art. [The first collection of his lyrics and his epic poems appeared at Wilna, in 1866, under the title ***Shire Yehudah.***] His poems of love are destitute of the personal note. On the other hand, in point of classic style and the modern polish of his verses, he outdistances all who preceded him. Lebensohn the younger removed from the arena, Gordon attained the first place among Hebrew poets.

In "David and Barzillai", the poet contrasts the tranquillity of the shepherd's life with that of the king. Gordon was happily inspired by the desire for outdoor life that had sprung up in the ghetto since Mapu's warm praise of rural scenes and pleasures, and also under the influence of the Jewish agricultural colonies founded in Russia. He shows us the aged king, crushed under a load of hardships, betrayed by his own son, standing face to face with the old shepherd, who refuses royal gifts.

"And David reigned as Israel's head,
And Barzillai his flocks to pasture led."

The charm of this little poem lies in the description of the land of Gilead. It seems that in reviving the past, the Hebrew poets were often vouchsafed remarkable insight into nature and local coloring, which ordinarily was not a characteristic of theirs. The same warmth and historical verisimilitude is found again in ***Asenath Bat-Potipherah***.

From the same period dates the first volume of fables by Gordon, published at Vienna, in 1860, under the title **Mishle Yehudah**, forming the second part of his collected poems, and being itself divided into four books. It consists of translations, or, better, imitations of Aesop, La Fontaine, and Kryloff, together with fables drawn from the Midrash. The style is concise and telling, and the satire is keen.

The production of these fables marks a turning-point in the work of Gordon. Snatched out of the indulgent and conciliatory surroundings in which he had developed, he found himself face to face with the sad reality of Jewish life in the provinces. The invincible fanaticism of the Rabbis, the anachronistic education given the children, who were kept in a state of ignorance, weighed heavily upon the heart of the patriot and man of intellect. It was the time in which liberal ideas and European civilization had penetrated into Russia under the protection of Czar Alexander II, and Gordon yearned to see his Russian co-religionists occupy a position similar to that enjoyed by their brethren in the West.

Those envied Jews of the West had had a proper understanding of the exigencies of their time. They had liberated themselves from the yoke of Rabbinism, and had assimilated with their fellow-citizens of other faiths. The Russian government encouraged the spread of education among the Jews, and granted privileges to such as profited by the opportunities offered. The reformers were strengthened also by the support of the newly-founded Hebrew journals. Gordon threw himself deliberately into the *fracas*. Poetry and prose, Hebrew and Russian, all served him to champion the cause of the Haskalah. With him the Haskalah was no longer limited to the cultivation of the Hebrew language and to the writing of philosophical treatises. It had become an undisguised conflict with obscurantism, ignorance, a time-worn routine, and all that barred the way to culture. Since the government permitted the Jews to enter the social life of the country, and seeing that they might in the future aspire to a better lot, the Haskalah should and would work to prepare them for it and make them worthy of it.

In 1863, after the liberation of the serfs in Russia, Gordon uttered a thrilling cry, **Hakizah 'Ammi!**

"Awake, O my people! How long wilt thou slumber? Lo, the night has vanished, the sun shines bright. Open thy eyes, look hither and thither. I pray thee, see in what place thou art, in what time thou livest!...

"The land wherein we were born, wherein we live, is it not part of Europe, the most civilized of all continents?...

"This land, Eden itself, behold, it is open unto thee, its sons welcome thee as brother.... Thou hast but to apply thy heart to wisdom and knowledge, become a public-spirited people, and speak their tongue!"

In another poem, the writer acclaims the dawn of a new time for the Jews. Their zeal to enter the liberal professions augurs well for a speedy and complete emancipation.

We have seen how stubborn a resistance was opposed by the orthodox to this new phase of the Haskalah. Terror seized upon them when they saw the young desert the religious schools and give themselves up to profane studies. As for the new Rabbinical seminaries, they regarded them as outright nurseries of atheism.

However, the government standing on the side of the reformers, the orthodox could not fight in the open. They entrenched themselves behind a passive resistance. In this struggle, as was observed above, Gordon occupied the foremost place. Thenceforth a single idea animated him, opposition to the enemies of light. His bitter, trenchant sarcasm, his caustic, vengeful pen, were put at the service of this cause. Even his historical poems quiver with his resentment. He loses no opportunity to scourge the Rabbis and their conservative adherents.

Ben Shinne Arayot ("Between the Teeth of the Lions") is an historical poem on a subject connected with the Judeo-Roman wars. The hero, Simon the Zealot, is taken captive by Titus. At the moment of succumbing in the arena, his eyes meet those of his beloved Martha, sold by the enemy as a slave, and the two expire at the same time.

The poem is a masterpiece by reason of the truly poetic inspiration that informs it, and the deep national feeling expressed in it. But Gordon did not stop at that. He makes use of the opportunity to attack Rabbinism in its vital beginnings, wherein he discerns the cause of his nation's peril.

> "Woe is thee, O Israel! Thy teachers have not taught thee how to conduct war with skill and strategem.

> "Rebellion and bravery, of what avail are they without discipline and tactics!

> "True, for many long centuries, they led thee, and constructed houses of learning for thee--but what did they teach thee?

> "What accomplished they? They but sowed the wind, and ploughed the rock, drew water in a sieve, and threshed empty straw!

> "They taught thee to run counter to life, to isolate thyself between walls of precepts and prescriptions, to be dead on earth and alive in heaven, to walk about in a dream and speak in thy sleep.

> "Thus thy spirit grew faint, thy strength dried up, and the dust of thy scribes has sepulchred thee, a living mummy....

> "Woe is thee, O Jerusalem that art lost!"

Yet, though he accuses Rabbinism of all possible ills that have befallen the Jewish people, it does not follow that he justifies the Roman invasion. All his wrath is aroused against Rome, the perennial enemy of Judaism. In the name of humanity and justice, he pours out his scorn over her. The first he presents is Titus, "the delight of mankind", preparing brilliant but sanguinary spectacles for his people, and revelling in the sight of innocent blood shed in the gladiators' arena. Then he arraigns Rome herself, "the great people who is mistress of three-quarters of the earth, the terror of the world, whose triumph can know no limit now that she has carried off the victory over a people destined to perish, whose territory can be covered in a five hours' march". And finally his Jewish heart is revolted by "the noble matrons followed by their servants, whose tender soul is about to take delight in the bloody sights of the arena".

Bi-Mezulot Yam ("In the Depths of the Sea") revives a terrible episode of the exodus of the Jews from Spain (1492). The refugees embarked on pirate vessels, where they were exploited pitilessly. The cupidity of the corsairs is insatiable. After despoiling the Jews of all they own, they sell them as slaves or cast them into the water. This is the lot that threatens to overtake a group of exiles on a certain ship. But the captain falls in love with the daughter of a Rabbi, a maiden of rare beauty. To rescue her companions, she pretends to yield to the solicitations of the captain, who promises to land the passengers safe and sound on the coast. He keeps his word, but the girl and her mother must stay with him. At a distance from the coast, the two women, with prayers to God upon their lips, throw themselves into the sea, to save the girl from having to surrender herself to the desires of the corsair. It is one of the most beautiful of Gordon's poems. Indignation and grief inspire such words as these:

> "The daughter of Jacob is banished from every foot of Spanish
> soil. Portugal also has thrust her out. Europe turns her back
> upon the unfortunates. She grants them only the grave, martyrdom,
> hell. Their bones are strewn upon the rocks of Africa. Their
> blood floods the shores of Asia.... And the Judge of the world
> appeareth not! And the tears of the oppressed are not avenged!"

What revolts the poet above all is the thought that the downtrodden victims will never have their revenge--all the crimes against them will go unpunished:

> "Never, O Israel, wilt thou be avenged! Power is with thy
> oppressors. What they desire they accomplish, what they do,
> prospereth.... Spain--did her vessels not set forth and discover
> the New World, the day thou wast driven out a fugitive and
> outlaw? And Portugal, did she not find the way to the Indies? And
> in that far-off country, too, she ruined the land that welcomed

thy refugees. Yea, Spain and Portugal stand unassailed!"

But if vengeance is withheld from the Jews, implacable hatred takes possession of all hearts, and never will it be appeased.

"Enjoin it upon your children until the end of days. Adjure your
descendants, the great and the little, never to return to the
land of Spain, reddened with your blood, never again to set foot
upon the Pyrenean peninsula!"

The despair, the grief of the poet are concentrated in the last stanzas, telling how the maiden and her mother throw themselves into the water:

"Only the Eye of the World, silently looking through the clouds,
the eye that witnesseth the end of all things, views the ruin of
these thousands of beings, and it sheds not a single tear."

His last historical poem, "King Zedekiah in Prison", dates from the period when the poet's skepticism was a confirmed temper of mind. According to Gordon, the ruin of the Jewish State was brought about by the weight given to moral as compared with political considerations. He no longer contents himself with attacking Rabbinism, he goes back to the very principles of the Judaism of the prophets. These are the ideas which he puts into the mouth of the King of Judah, the captive of Nebuchadnezzar. He makes him the advocate of the claims of political power as against the moralist pretensions of the prophets.

The king passes all his misfortunes in review, and he asks himself to what cause they are attributable.

"Because I did not submit to the will of Jeremiah? But what was
it that the priest of Anathoth required of me to do?"

No, the king cannot concede that "the City would still be standing if her inhabitants had not borne burdens on the Sabbath day".

The prophet proclaims the rule of the letter and of the Law, supreme over work and war, but can a people of dreamers and visionaries exist a single day?

The king does not stop at such rebellious thoughts. He remembers all too well the story of Saul and Samuel--how the king was castigated for having resisted the whims of the prophets.

"Thus the seers and prophets have always sought to crush the kings in Israel", he maintains.

"Alas! I see that the words of the son of Hilkiah will be fulfilled without fail. The Law will stand, the kingdom will be ruined. The book, the word--they will succeed to the royal sceptre. I foresee a whole people of scholars and teachers, degenerate folk and feeble."

This amazing view, so disconcerting to the prophet-people, Gordon held to the very end. And seeing that the Law had killed the nation, and a cruel fatality dogged the footsteps of the people of the Book, would it not be best to free the individuals from the chains of the faith and liberate the masses from the minute religious ceremonial that has obstructed their path to life? This was the task Gordon set himself for the rest of his days.

In a poem inscribed to Smolenskin, the editor of ***Ha-Shahar*** ("Daybreak"), on the occasion of the periodical's resuming publication after an interval, the poet poured forth his afflicted soul, and pointed out the aim he had decided to pursue:

"Once upon a time I sang of love, too, and pleasure, and friendship; I announced the advent of days of joy, liberty, and hope. The strings of my lyre thrilled with emotion....

"But yonder comes ***Ha-Shahar*** again, and I shall attune my harp to hail the break of day.

"Alas, I am no more the same, I know not how to sing, I waken naught but grief. Disquieting dreams trouble my nights. They show me my people face to face.... They show me my people in all its abasement, with all its unprobed wounds. They reveal to me the iniquity that is the source of all its ills.

"I see its leaders go astray, and its teachers deceiving it. My heart bleeds with grief. The strings of my lyre groan, my song is a lament.

"Since that day I sing no more of joy and solace; I hope no more for the light, I wait no more for liberty. I sing only of bitter days, I foretell everlasting slavery, degradation, and no end. And from the strings of my lyre tears gush forth for the ruin of my people.

"Since that day my muse is black as a raven, her mouth is filled with abuse, from her tongue drops complaint. She groans like the Bat-Kol upon Mount Horeb's ruins. She cries out against the wicked shepherds, against the sottish people.

"She recounts unto God, unto all the human kind, the degrading miseries of a hand-to-mouth existence, of the soul that pierces to the depths of evil."
But the patriotism of the poet carries the day over his discouragement:

"From pity for my people, from compassion, I will tell unto its shepherds their crimes, unto its teachers the error of their ways."

Will he succeed in his purpose? Is not all hope lost? No matter, he at least will do his duty until the end:

"From every part of the Law, from every retreat of the people, I shall gather together all vain teachings, all the poisonous

vipers, wherever they may be, and in the sight of all suspend
them like a banner. Let the wounded look upon them, perhaps they
will be cured--perhaps there is still healing for their ills,
perhaps there is still life in them!"

The poet kept his word. In a series of satires, fables, and epistles, he reveals the moral plagues that eat into the fabric of Jewish society in the Slav countries. He gives a realistic description, at once accurate and subjective, of an extraordinary *milieu*, lacking plausibility though it existed and defied all opposition. Gordon descended to the innermost depths of the people's soul, he knew its profoundest secrets. He caught the spirit of the peculiar manners of the ghetto and reproduced them with unfailing fidelity. Also he knew all the dishonor of some of the persons who ruled its society, and he sounded their mean, crafty brains. His heart was filled with indignation at the painful spectacle he himself bodied forth, and he suffered the misfortunes of his people.

His poetic manner changed with the new direction taken by his mind. He was no more an artist for art's sake. Classical purity ceased to interest him. What he pursued above all things was an object which can be reached only by struggle and propaganda. His style became more realistic. He saturated it with Talmudic terms and phrases, thus adapting it more closely to the spirit of the scenes and things and acts he was occupied with, and making it the proper medium for the description of a world that was Rabbinical in all essential points. But Gordon never went to excess in the use of Talmudisms; he always maintained a just sense of proportion. It requires discriminating taste to appreciate his style, now delicate and now sarcastic, by turns appealing and vehement. Here Gordon displayed the whole range of his talent, all his creative powers. The language he uses is the genuine modern Hebrew, a polished and expressive medium, yielding in naught to the classical Hebrew.

The social condition of the Jewish woman, the saddest conceivable in the ghetto, inspired the first of Gordon's satires. The poem is entitled "The Dot on the I", or, more literally, "The Hanger of the Yod" (**Kozo shel Yod**).

"O thou, Jewish Woman, who knows thy life! Unnoticed thou
enterest the world, unnoticed thou departest from it.

"Thy heart-aches and thy joys, thy sorrows and thy desires spring up within thee and die within thee.

"All the good things of this life, its pleasures, its enjoyments, they were created for the daughters of the other nations. The Jewish woman's life is naught but servitude, toil without end. Thou conceivest, thou bearest, thou givest suck, thou weanest thy babes, thou bakest, thou cookest, and thou witherest before thy time."

"Vain for thee to be dowered with an impressionable heart, to be beautiful, gentle, intelligent!"

"The Law in thy mouth is turned to foolishness, beauty in thee is a taint, every gift a fault, all knowledge a defect.... Thou art but a hen good to raise a brood of chicks!"

It is vain for a Jewish woman to cherish aspirations after life, after knowledge--nothing of all this is accessible to her.

"The planting of the Lord wastes away in a desert land without having seen the light of the sun...."

"Before thou becomest conscious of thy soul, before thou knowest aught, thou art given in marriage, thou art a mother."

"Before thou hast learnt to be a daughter to thy parents, thou art a wife, and mother to children of thine own."

"Thou art betrothed--knowest thou him for whom thou art destined? Dost thou love him? Yea, hast thou seen him?--Love! Thou unhappy being! Knowest thou not that to the heart of a Jewish woman love is prohibited?"

> "Forty days before thy birth, thy mate and life companion was assigned to thee." [1]

> "Cover thy head, cut off thy braids of hair. Of what avail to look at him who stands beside thee? Is he hunchbacked or one-eyed? Is he young or old? What matters it? Not thou hast chosen, but thy parents, they rule over thee, like merchandise thou passest from hand to hand."

[1: According to popular belief, it is decided forty days before its birth to whom a child will be married.]

Slave to her parents, slave to her husband, she is not permitted to taste even the joys of motherhood in peace. Unforeseen misfortunes assail her and lay her low. Her husband, without an education, without a profession, often without a heart, finds himself suddenly at odds with life, after having eaten at the table and lodged in the house of his wife's parents for a number of years following his marriage, as is customary among the Jews of the Slavic countries. If no chance of success presents itself soon, he grows weary, abandons his wife and children, and goes off no one knows whither, without a sign of his whereabouts, and she remains behind, an ***'Agunah***, a forsaken wife, widowed without being a widow, most unfortunate of unfortunate creatures.

> "This is the history of all Jewish women, and it is the history of Bath-shua the beautiful."

Bath-shua is a noble creature, endowed by nature with all fine qualities--she is beautiful, intelligent, pure, good, attractive, and an excellent housekeeper. She is admired by everybody. Even the miserable ***Parush***, the recluse student, conceals himself behind the railing that divides the women's gallery from the rest of the synagogue, to steal a look at her. Alas, this flower of womankind is betrothed by her father to a certain Hillel, a sour specimen, ugly, stupid, repulsive. But he knows the Talmud by heart, folio by folio, and to say that is to say everything. The marriage comes off in due time, the young couple eat at the table of Bath-shua's parents for three years, and two children spring from the union.

The wife's father loses his fortune, and Hillel must earn his own livelihood. Incapable as he is, he finds nothing to do, and he goes to foreign parts to seek his fortunes. Never is he heard of again. Bath-shua remains behind alone with her two children. By painful toil, she earns her bread with unfailing courage. All the love of her rich nature she pours out upon her children, whom by a supreme effort she dresses and adorns like the children of the wealthy.

Meantime a young man by the name of Fabi makes his appearance in the little town. He is the type of the modern Jew, educated and intelligent, and he is handsome and generous besides. He begins by taking an interest in the young woman, and ends by falling in love with her. Bath-shua does not dare believe in her happiness. But an insurmountable obstacle lies in the path of their union. Bath-shua is not divorced from her husband, and none can tell whether he is dead or alive. Energetically Fabi undertakes to find the hiding-place of the faithless man. He traces him, and bribes him to give his wife a divorce. The official document, properly drawn up and attested by a Rabbinical authority, is sent to her. Hillel embarks for America, and his vessel suffers shipwreck.

Finally, it would seem, Bath-shua will enjoy the happiness she has amply merited. Alas, no! In the person of Rabbi Wofsi, fortune plays her another trick. This Rabbi is a rigid legalist, the slightest of slips suffices to render the divorce invalid. According to certain commentators the name Hillel is spelled incorrectly in the document. After the **He** a **Yod** is missing! Thus is the happiness glimpsed by Bath-shua shattered forever!

Her fate is not unique--the Bath-shuas are counted by the legion in the ghetto. And there are other fates no less poignant caused by reasons no less futile.

In another poem, ***Ashakka de-Rispak*** ("The Shaft of the Wagon", meaning "For a Trifle"), the poet tells how the peace of a household was undermined on account of a barley grain discovered by accident in the soup at the Passover meal, which must be free from every trace of fermented food. Brooding over the incident and filled with remorse for having served the doubtful soup to her family, the poor woman runs to the Rabbi, who decides that she has, indeed, caused her family to eat prohibited food, and the dishes in which it was prepared and served must be broken, they cannot be used, they may not even be sold. But the husband, a simple carter, does not accept the decision tranquilly. He vents his anger upon the woman. The peace of the house is troubled, and finally the man repudiates his wife.

The poet fulminates against the Rabbis and their narrow, senseless interpretations of texts.

> "Slaves we were in the land of Egypt.... And what are we now? Do we not sink lower from year to year? Are we not bound with ropes of absurdities, with cords of quibbles, with all sorts of prejudices?... The stranger no longer oppresses us, our despots are the progeny of our own bodies. Our hands are no longer manacled, but our soul is in chains."

In the last of his great satires, "The Two Joseph-ben-Simons", Gordon gives a sombre and at the same time lofty picture of the manners of the ghetto, an exact description of the wicked, arbitrary domination exercised by the **Kahal**, and an idealization of the Maskil, powerless to prevail single-handed in the combat with combined reactionary forces. A young Talmudist, devotee of the sciences and of modern literature, is persecuted by the fanatics. Unable to resist the seductions of his alien studies, he is forced to expatriate himself. He goes to Italy, to the University of Padua, whither the renown of Samuel David Luzzatto has attracted many a young Russian Jew eager for knowledge. There he pursues both Rabbinical and medical courses.

His efforts are crowned with success, and he dreams of returning to his country and consecrating his powers to the amelioration of the material and moral condition of his brethren. In his mind's eye he sees himself at the head of his community, healing souls and bodies, redressing wrongs, introducing reforms, breathing a new spirit into the dry bones and limbs of Judaism. Hardly has he set foot upon the soil of his native town when he is arrested and thrown into prison. The Kahal had made out a passport in his name for the cobbler's son, a degraded character, a highway robber and sneak thief, and charged with murder. Now the true Joseph ben Simon is to expiate the crime of the other. It is vain for him to protest his innocence. The president of the Kahal, before whom he is arraigned, declares there is no other Joseph ben Simon, and he is the guilty one.

The little town is described minutely. We are on the public square, the market place, the dumping ground of all the offal and dirt, whence an offensive odor rises in the nostrils of the passer-by. Facing this square is the synagogue, a mean, dilapidated building. "Mud and filth detract from holiness", but the Lord takes no offense, "He thrones too high to be incommoded by it". The greatest impurity, however, a moral infection, oozes from the little chamber adjoining the synagogue--the meeting-room of the Kahal. That is the breeding place of crime and injustice. Oppression and venality assert themselves there with barefaced impudence. The Kahal keeps the lists relating to military service; it makes out the passports, and the whole town is at its mercy. It offers the hypocrite of the ghetto the opportunity of exercising his fatal power. There the widow is despoiled, and the orphans are abused. Together with the unfortunates who have dared aspire to the light, the fatherless are delivered to the recruiting agent as substitutes for the sons of the wealthy. It is the domain over which reigns the venerated Rabbi, powerful and fear-inspiring, Shamgar ben Anath, a stupid and uncouth upstart.

The life of sacrifices and privations led by the Jewish students who go abroad in search of an education, inspires Gordon with one of the most beautiful passages in his poem. In the true sense of the word, these young men are loyal to Jewish traditions. They are the genuine successors of those who formerly braved hunger and cold upon the benches of the *Yeshibot*.

> "How strong it is, the desire for knowledge in the hearts of the
> youth of Israel, the crushed people! It is like the fire, never
> extinguished, burning upon the altar!...
>
> "Stop upon the highways leading to Mir, Eisheshok, and Wolosin.
> [1] See yon haggard youths walking on foot! Whither lead their
> steps? What do they seek?--Naked they will sleep upon the floor,
> and lead a life of privation.
>
> "It is said: 'The Torah is given to him alone who dies for her!'"
> [1: Lithuanian towns well-known for their Talmudic academies.]
> And here is the modern counterpart:

"Go to no matter what university in Europe: the lot of the young Jewish strangers is no better.... The Russians are proud of the fame of a Lomonossoff, the son of a poor moujik who became a luminary in the world of science. How numerous are the Lomonossoffs of the Jew alley!..."
And then the poet, in an access of patriotism, cries out:

"And what, in fine, art thou, O Israel, but a poor **Bahur** among the peoples, eating one day with one of them, another day with the other!...

"Thou hast kindled a perpetual lamp for the whole world. Around thee alone the world is dark, O People, slave of slaves, desperate and despised!"

With this poem we bring to a close the analysis of Gordon's satires. It shows at their best the dreams, the aspirations, the struggles of the Maskilim, in their opposition to the aims of the reactionaries and the moral and material confusion in which Slavic Judaism wallowed.

The same order of ideas is presented in the greater part of the original pieces in his "Little Fables for Big Children". They are written in a vivid, pithy style. The delicate, bantering criticism and the deep philosophy with which they are impregnated put these fables among the finest productions of Hebrew literature.

To the same period as the fables belong the several volumes of tales published by Gordon, **Shene Yomim we-Lailah Ehad** ("Two Days and One Night"), **'Olam ke-Minhago** ("The World as It is"), and later the first part of **Kol Kitbe Yehudah** ("Collected Writings of Gordon"). They also relate to the life and manners of the Jews of Lithuania, and the struggle of the modern element with the old. Gordon as story teller is inferior to Gordon as poet. Nevertheless his prose displays all the delicacy of his mind and the precision of his observations. At all events, these tales of his are not a negligible quantity in Hebrew literature.

The reaction which set in about 1870, after a period of social reforms and unrealized hopes, affected the poet deeply. The government put obstacles in the forward march of the Jews, the masses remained steeped in fanaticism, and the men of light and leading themselves fell short of doing their whole duty. Disillusioned, he cherished no hope of anything. He could not share the optimism of Smolenskin and his school. For an instant he stops to look back over the road travelled. He sees nothing, and in anguish he asks himself:

"For whom have I toiled all the years of my prime?

"My parents, they cling to the faith and to their people, they think of nothing but business and religious observances all day long; they despise knowledge, and are hostile to good sense....

"Our intellectuals scorn the national language, and all their love is lavished upon the language of the land.

"Our daughters, charming as they are, are kept in absolute ignorance of Hebrew....

"And the young generation go on and on, God knows how far and whither ... perhaps to the point whence they will never return."

He therefore addresses himself to a handful of the elect, amateurs, the only ones who do not despise the Hebrew poet, but understand him and approve his ways:

"To you I bring my genius as a sacrifice, before you I shed my tears as a libation.... Who knows but I am the last to sing of Zion, and you the last to read the Zion songs?"

This pessimistic strain recurs in all the later writings of Gordon. Even after the events of 1882, when revived hatred and persecution had thrown the camp of the emancipators into disorder, and the most ardent of the anti-Rabbinic champions, like Lilienblum and Braudes, had been driven to the point of raising the flag of Zionism, Gordon alone of all was not carried along with the current. His skepticism kept him from embracing the illusions of his friends converted to Zionism.

All his contempt for the tyrants, and his compassion for his people unjustly oppressed, he puts into his poem ***Ahoti Ruhamah***, which is inscribed "to the Honor of the Daughter of Jacob violated by the Son of Hamor."

"Why weepest thou, my afflicted sister?

"Wherefore this desolation of spirit, this anguish of heart?

"If thieves surprised thee and ravished thy honor, if the hand of
the malefactor has prevailed against thee, is it thy fault, my
afflicted sister?

"Whither shall I bear my shame?

"Where is thy shame, seeing thy heart is pure and chaste? Arise,
display thy wound, that all the world may see the blood of Abel
upon the forehead of Cain. Let the world know, my afflicted
sister, how thou art tortured!

"Not upon thee falls the shame, but upon thy oppressors.

"Thy purity has not been sullied by their polluting touch....
Thou art white as snow, my afflicted sister."

Almost the poet seems to regret his efforts of other days to bring the Jews close to the Christians.

"What of humiliation hath befallen thee is a solace unto me. Long
I bore distress and injustice, violence and spoliation; yet I
remained loyal to my country; for better days I hoped, and

submitted to all. But to bear thy shame, my afflicted sister, I
have no spirit more."

But what was to become of it all? Whither were the Jews to turn? The Palestine of the Turk has not too many attractions for the poet. He still believes in the existence of a country somewhere "in which the light shines for all human beings alike, in which man is not humiliated on account of his race or his faith." Thither he invites his brethren to go and seek an asylum, "until what day our Father in heaven will take pity on us and return us to our ancient mother."

It was the agitated time in which Pinsker sent forth his manifesto, "Auto-Emancipation", and Gordon dedicated his poem, "The Flock of the Lord", to him.

"What are we, you ask, and what our life? Are we a people like
those around us, or only members of a religious community? I will
tell you: We are neither a people, nor a brotherhood, we are but
a flock--the holy flock of the Lord God, and the whole earth is
an altar for us. Thereon we are laid either as burnt offerings
sacrificed by the other peoples, or as victims bound by the
precepts of our own Rabbis. A flock wandering in the waste
desert, sheep set upon on all sides by the wolves.... We cry out--
in vain! We utter laments--none hears! The desert shuts us in on
all sides. The earth is of copper, the heavens are of brass.

"Not an ordinary flock are we, but a flock of iron. We survive
the slaughter. But will our strength endure forever?

"A flock dispersed, undisciplined, without a bond--we are the
flock of the Lord God!"

Not that the idea of a national rebirth displeased the poet. Far from it. Zionism cannot but exercise a charm upon the Jewish heart. But he believed the time had not yet arrived for a national regeneration. According to his opinion, there was a work of religious liberation to be accomplished before the reconstruction of the

Jewish State could be thought of. He defended this idea in a series of articles published in ***Ha-Meliz***, of which he was the editor at that time.

The last years of his life were tragic, pathetic. With a torn heart he sat by and looked upon the desperate situation into which the government had put millions of his brethren. To this he alludes in his fable "Adoni-bezek", which we reproduce in its entirety, to give a notion of Gordon as a fabulist:

> "In a sumptuous palace, in the middle of a vast hall, perfumed, and draped with Egyptian fabrics, stands a table, and upon it are the most delicious viands. Adoni-bezek is dining. His attendants are standing each in his place--his cupbearer, the master baker, and the chief cook. The eunuchs, his slaves, come and go; bringing every variety of dainty dishes, and the flesh of all sorts of beasts and birds, roasted and stewed.

> "On the floor, insolent dogs lie sprawling, their jaws agape, panting to snap up the bones and scraps their master throws to them.

> "Prostrate under the table are seventy captive kings, with their thumbs and big toes cut off. To appease their appetite they must scramble for the scraps that drop under the table of their sovereign lord.

> "Adoni-bezek has finished his repast, and he amuses himself with throwing bones to the creatures under the table. Suddenly there is a hubbub, the dogs bark, and yap at their human neighbors, who have appropriated morsels meant for them.

> "The wounded kings complain to the master: O king, see our suffering and deliver us from thy dogs. And Adoni-bezek's answer is: But it is you who are to be blamed, and they are in the right. Why do you do them wrong?

"With bitterness the kings make reply:

"O king, is it our fault if we have been brought so low that we must vie with your dogs and pick up the crumbs that drop from your table? Thou didst come up against us and crush us with thy powerful hand, thou didst mutilate us and chain us in these cages. No longer are we able to work or seek our sustenance. Why should these dogs have the right to bite and bark? O that the just--if still there are such men in our time--might rise up! O that one whose heart has been touched by God might judge between ourselves and those who bite us, which of us is the hangman and which the victim?"

Toward the end of his days the poet was permitted to enjoy a great gratification. The Jewish notabilities of the capital arranged a celebration of the twenty-fifth anniversary of his activity as a writer. At the reunion of Gordon's friends on this occasion it was decided to publish an ***edition de luxe*** of his poetical works. A final optimistic note was forced from his heart, deeply moved by this unexpected tribute. He recalled the vow once made by him, always to remain loyal to Hebrew, and he recounted the vexations and disappointments to which the poet is exposed who chooses to write in a dead language doomed to oblivion. Then he addressed a salutation to the young "of whom we had despaired, and who are coming back, and to the dawn of the rebirth of the Hebrew language and the Jewish people."

However, Gordon never entered into the national revival with full faith in its promises. Until the end he remained the poet of misery and despair.

The death of Smolenskin elicited a last disconsolate word from him. It may be considered the ghetto poet's testament. He compared the great writer to the Jewish people, and asked himself:

"What is our people, and what its literature?
A giant felled to the ground unable to rise.
The whole earth is its sepulchre.
And its books?--the epitaph engraved upon its tomb-stone...."

CHAPTER VIII
REFORMERS AND CONSERVATIVES
THE TWO EXTREMES

Though Gordon was the most distinguished, he was not the only representative of the anti-Rabbinic school in the neo-Hebrew literature. The decline of liberalism in official state circles, and the frustration of every hope of equality, had their effect in reshaping the policy pursued by educated Jews. Up to this time they had cherished no desire except for external emancipation and to assimilate with their neighbors of other faiths. Liberty and justice suddenly removed from their horizon, they could not but transfer their ambition and their activity to the inner chambers of Judaism. Other circumstances contributed to the result. The economic changes affecting the bourgeoisie and the influence exercised by the realism and the utilitarian tendencies of the Russian literature of the time had not a little to do with the modified aims cherished in the camp of the Maskilim. Jews of education living in Galicia or in the small towns of Russia, who had the best opportunity of penetrating to the intimate life of the people and knowing its day by day misery, could and did make clear, how helpless the masses of the Jews were in the face of the moral and economic ruin that menaced them, and how serious an obstacle religious restrictions and ignorance placed in the way of any change in their condition. And therefore they made it their object to extol practical, thoroughgoing reforms.

In religion, they demanded, with Gordon, the abolition of all restrictions weighing upon the people, and a radical reform of Jewish education.

In practical life, they were desirous of turning the attention of their brethren to the manual trades, to the technical professions, and to agriculture. Besides, it was their purpose to extend modern primary instruction and bring it within the reach of considerably larger circles.

The government viewed these efforts with a favorable eye, and under its protection the Society for the Promotion of Culture among the Jews in Russia was formed, with headquarters at St. Petersburg. Thus supported, the educated could carry on their propaganda in the open, and throw light into the remotest corners of the country. The Hebrew press, though still in its infancy, co-operated with them zealously in furthering their beneficent purposes.

The most determined group of the anti-religious propagandists was at Brody in Galicia. Thence emanated the influences that operated in Russia, and thence **He-Haluz** ("The Pioneer"), founded by Erter and Schorr in 1853, and published at Lemberg, carried on a brilliant campaign against religious superstitions, shrinking not even from attacks upon the Biblical tradition itself. The boldest of the contributors to **He-Haluz**, not counting its valiant editor, was Abraham Krochmal, the son of the philosopher. A scholar and subtle thinker, he introduced Biblical criticism into Hebrew literature. In his books as well as in his articles in **He-Haluz** and in **Ha-Kol**, the latter edited by Rodkinson, he goes so far as to dispute the Divine character of the Bible, and he demands radical reforms in Judaism. [**Ha-Ketab weha-Miktab** ("Writing and the Scriptures"), Lemberg, 1875; *'Iyyun Tefillah* ("Reflections on Prayer"), Lemberg, 1885, etc.] His writings gave the signal for a considerable stir and expression of opinion. Even the most moderate among the orthodox could not remain tranquil in the presence of such blasphemous views. They put Krochmal outside of the pale of Judaism, together with all scholars occupied with Bible criticism, among them Geiger, who had exerted great influence upon the school of reformers writing in Hebrew.

In Lithuania things did not go so far. The hard conditions of existence there were not propitious to the rise of a purely scholarly school or to theoretic discussion. Scientific centres were entirely wanting, and the censor permitted no trifling with the subject of religion. A new movement, realistic and utilitarian in the main, began to take shape, first in the form of a protest against the unsubstantial ideals of the Hebrew press and Hebrew literature. In 1867, Abraham Kowner, an ardent controversialist, published his **Heker Dabar** ("A Word of Criticism"), and his **Zeror Perahim** ("A Bouquet of Flowers"), in which he takes the press and the writers severely to task for indulging in rhetoric and futile scintillations, instead of occupying themselves with the real exigencies of life. In the same year, Abraham Jacob Paperna published his essay in literary criticism, and the young Smolenskin, in an article appearing at Odessa, attacked Letteris for his artificial, insincere translation of Goethe's *Faust* into Hebrew. On all sides there blew a fresh breath of realism, and the critical spirit was abroad.

The most characteristic exponent of this reforming movement was Moses Lob Lilienblum, a native of the Government of Kowno. Endowed with a temperate, logical mind, untroubled by an excess of sentimentality, Lilienblum, one of those deliberate, puritanic scholars that constitute the glory of Lithuanian Talmudism, was at once hero and actor in the intense drama performed in the Russian ghetto, which he himself described as the "Jewish tragi-comedy".

He began his literary career with an article entitled ***Orhot ha- Talmud*** ("The Paths of the Talmud"), and published in ***Ha-Meliz*** in 1868. Here, as well as in the articles following it, he does not depart from established tradition. In the very name of the spirit of the Talmud, he demands religious reforms and the abolition of the restrictions that make daily life burdensome. These excessive requirements, he urges, were heaped up by the Rabbis subsequent to the full development of the Law, and in opposition to its spirit. The young scholar showed himself to be a zealous admirer of the Talmud, and with clinching logic he proves that the Rabbis of later times, in asserting its immutability, had distinctly deviated from the principles of the Law, the fundamental idea of which was the harmonizing of "Law and Life". The wrath aroused by such articles can easily be imagined. Lilienblum was an ***Apikoros***, the "heretic" ***par excellence*** of the Lithuanian ghetto. The young writer had to undergo a series of outrageous persecutions and acts of vengeance inflicted by the fanatics, especially the Hasidim, of his town. He tells the story in detail in his autobiography, ***Hattot Neurim*** ("The Sins of Youth"), published at Vienna, in 1876, one of the most noteworthy productions of modern Hebrew literature. With the logical directness of a ***Mitnagged*** [1], and the cruel, sarcastic candor of a wasted existence, Lilienblum probes and exposes the depths of his tortured conscience, at the same time following up inexorably the steps which remove the free-thinker from the faithful believer, without, however, reaching a real or positive result-- in the spirit at once of Rousseau and Voltaire. [Footnote 1: Literally, "one who is opposed" [to the mystical system of Hasidism]; a protestant, a Puritan.] As he himself says:

> "It is a drama essentially Jewish, because it is a life without
> dramatic effect, without extraordinary adventure. It is made up
> of torment and suffering, all the more grievous as they are kept
> hidden in the recesses of one's heart...."

Better than any one else he knows the cause of these ills. Like Gordon, he holds that the Book has killed the Man, the dead letter has been substituted for feeling.

> "You ask me, O reader", he says with bitterness, "who I am, and
> what my name is?--Well, then, I am a living being, not a Job who
> has never existed. Nor am I one of the dead in the valley of
> bones brought back to life by the prophet Ezekiel, which is only
> a tale that is told. But I am one of the living dead of the
> Babylonian Talmud, revived by the new Hebrew literature, itself a
> dead literature, powerless to bring the dead to life with its
> dew, scarcely able to transport us into a state between life and
> death. I am a Talmudist, a believer aforetimes, now become an
> unbeliever, no longer clinging to the dreams and the hopes which
> my ancestors bequeathed to me. I am a wreck, a miserable wretch,
> hopeless unto despair...."

And he narrates the incidents of his childhood, the period of the *Tohu*, of chaos and confusion, the days of study, misery, superstition. He recalls the years of adolescence, his premature marriage, his struggle for a bare existence, his wretched life as a teacher of the Talmud, panting under the double yoke of a mother-in-law and a rigid ceremonial. Then comes his introduction to Hebrew literature. His conscience long refuses assent, but stern logic triumphs, and the result is that all the ideas that have been his guiding principles crumble into dust one by one. Negation replaces faith. The terrible conflict begins with a whole town of formalists, who declare him outside of the community of Israel,--a pitiless conflict, in which he is supported half-heartedly by two or three of the strong- minded. The publication of his first article, on the necessity of reforms in religion, increases the fury of the people against him, and his ruin is determined. Had there not been intervention from the outside, he would have been delivered to the authorities to serve in the army, or denounced as a dangerous heretic. And yet the so-called heretic cursed by every mouth had proceeded so short a distance on the path of heterodoxy that he still entertained scruples about carrying a book from one house to another on the Sabbath!

This naive soul, in which all sorts of feelings had long before begun to stir obscurely, was aroused to full consciousness by the reading of Mapu's works. Casual acquaintance with an intelligent woman made his heart vibrate with notes unknown until then. Life in his native town became intolerable, and he left it for Odessa, the El Dorado of all ghetto dreamers. Again disillusionment was his lot. He who was ready to undergo martyrdom for his ideas, this champion of the Haskalah, his heart famishing for knowledge and justice, was not long in discerning, with his penetrating, perspicacious mind, that he had not yet reached the best of modern worlds. With bitterness he notes that the Jews of the south of Russia, "where the Talmud is cut out of practical life, if they are more liberal than the others, are yet not exempt from stupid superstitions." He notes that the Hebrew literature so dear to his heart is excluded from the circles of the intellectual. He sees that egotistic materialism has superseded the ideal aspirations of the ghetto. He discovers that feeling has no place in modern life, and tolerance, the loudly vaunted, is but a sound. When he ventures to put his complaints into words, he is treated as a "religious fanatic" by people who have no interest beyond their own selfish pleasures and the satisfaction of their material cravings. He is deeply affected by what he observes and notes. In the presence of the egotistic indifference of the emancipated Jews, he is shaken in his firmest convictions, and he admits with anguish that the ideal for which he has fought and sacrificed his life is but a phantom. Under the stress of such disappointment he writes these lines:

> "In very truth, I tell you, never will the Jewish religion be in
> accord with life. It will sink, or, at best, it will remain the
> cherished possession of the limited few, as it is now in the
> Western countries of Europe.... Practical reality is in
> opposition to religion. Now I know that we have no public on our

side; and actual life with its great movements produces its results without the aid of literature, which even in our people is an effective influence only with the simple spirits of the country districts. The desire for life and liberty, the prevalence of charlatanism on the one side, and on the other the abandoning of religious studies in favor of secular studies, will have baleful consequences for the Jewish youth, even in Lithuania."

This whole period of our author's life is characterized by similar regrets--he mourns over days spent in barren struggles and over the follies of youth.

"To-day I finished writing my autobiography, which I call 'The Sins of Youth'. I have drawn up the balance-sheet of my life of thirty years and one month, and I am deeply grieved to see that the sum total is a cipher. How heavily the hand of fortune has lain upon me! The education I received was the reverse of everything I had need of later. I was raised with the idea of becoming a distinguished Rabbinical authority, and here I am a business man; I was raised in an imaginary world, to be a faithful observer of the Law, shrinking back from whatever has the odor of sin, and the very things I was taught crush me to earth now that the imaginary man has disappeared in me; I was raised to live in the atmosphere of the dead, and here I am cast among people who lead a real life, in which I am unable to take my part; I was raised in a world of dreams and pure theory, and I find myself now in the midst of the chaos of practical life, to which I am driven by my needs to apply myself, though my brain refuses to leave the old ruts and substitute practice for speculation. I am not even equipped to carry on a discussion with business men discussing nothing but business. I was raised to be the father of a family, in the sphere chosen for me by my father in his wisdom.... How far removed my heart is from all such things...!

"I weep over my shattered little world which I cannot restore!"

The regrets of Lilienblum over the useless work attempted by Hebrew literature betray themselves also in his pamphlet in verse, **Kehal Refaim** ("The Assembly of the Dead"). The dead are impersonated by the Hebrew periodicals and reviews.

Later, a novelist of talent, Reuben Asher Braudes, resumed the attempt to harmonize theory and practice, in his great novel, "Religion and Life". The hero, the young Rabbi Samuel, is the picture of Lilienblum. From the point of view of art, it is one of the best novels in Hebrew literature. Life in the rural districts, the austere idealism of the enlightened, the superstitions of the crowd, are depicted with extraordinary clearness of outline. [**Ha-Dat weha- Hayyim**, Lemberg, 1880. Another long novel by Braudes is called **Shete ha-Kezawot** ("The Two Extremes"), published in 1886, wherein he extols the national revival and religious romanticism.] The novel ran in **Ha-Boker Or** (1877-1880), and was never completed--a counterpart of its hero. Had not Lilienblum, too, stopped in the middle of the road?

The crisis that occurred in the life of Lilienblum, torn from his ideal speculations in a provincial town, and forced into contact with an actuality that was as far as possible away from solving the problem of harmonizing religion and life, was the typical fate of all the educated Jews of the period. Lilienblum and his followers gave themselves up to regrets over the futile work of three generations of humanists, who, instead of restoring the ghetto to health, had but hastened its utter ruin. The ideal aspirations of the Maskilim had been succeeded by a gross utilitarianism without an ideal. What disquieted the soul of the Maskil in the decade from 1870 to 1880 is expressed in the concluding words of "The Sins of Youth":

"The young people are to work at nothing and think of nothing but
how to prepare for their own life. All is forbidden, wherefrom
they cannot derive direct profit--they are permitted only the
study of sciences and languages, or apprenticeship to a trade.

"The youth who break away from the laborious study of the Talmud,

throw themselves with avidity into the study of modern
literature. This headlong course has been in vogue with us about
a century. One generation disappears, to make place for the next,
and each generation is pushed forward by a blind force, no one
knows whither...!

"It is high time for us to throw a glance backward--to stop a
moment and ask ourselves: Whither are we hastening, and why do we
hasten?"....

However, the gods did not forsake the ghetto. If Gordon and, with more emphasis, Lilienblum predicted the ruin of all the dreams of the ghetto, it was because, having been wrenched from the life of the masses and out of traditional surroundings, they judged things from a distance, and permitted themselves to be influenced by appearances. Blinded by their bias, they saw only two well-defined camps in Judaism--the moderns, indifferent to all that constitutes Judaism, and the bigots, opposed to what savors of knowledge, free-thinking, and worldly pleasure. They made their reckoning without the Jewish people. The humanist propaganda was not so empty and vain as its later promoters were pleased to consider it. The conservative romanticism of a Samuel David Luzzatto and the Zionist sentiments of a Mapu had planted a germinating seed in the heart of traditional Judaism itself. It is conceded that we cannot resort for evidence to such old romanticists as Schulman, who in the serenity of their souls gave little heed to the campaign of the reformers, though it is nevertheless a fact that they contributed to the diffusion of humanism and of Hebrew literature by their works, which were well received in orthodox circles. Our contention is better proved by Rabbis reputed orthodox, who devoted themselves with enthusiasm to the cultivation of Hebrew literature. Without renouncing religion, they found a way of effecting the harmonization of religion and life. In point of fact, humanism of a conservative stripe reached its zenith at the precise moment when the realists, deceived by superficial appearances, were predicting the complete breaking up of traditional Judaism.

The chief representatives of the reform press were ***He-Haluz***, ***Ha-Meliz***, and later on ***Ha-Kol*** ("The Voice"), and by their side the views of the conservatives were defended in ***Ha-Maggid***, ***Ha-Habazzelet*** ("The Lily"), published at Jerusalem, and especially ***Ha-Lebanon***, appearing first at Paris and then at Mayence. In ***Ha-Maggid***, beginning with the year 1871, the editor, David Gordon, supported by the assenting opinion of his readers, carried on an ardent campaign for the colonization of Palestine as the necessary forerunner of the political revival of Israel.

A Galician thinker, Fabius Mises, published, in 1869, an article in ***Ha-Meliz***, entitled ***Milhemet ha-Dat*** ("The Wars of the Faith"), in which he wards off the attacks upon the Jewish religion by the anti-Rabbinical school. He proves it to be a reasonable religion, and a national religion *par excellence*. In his poems, Mises assails Geiger for the religious reforms urged by him, and he opposes also the school of ***He-Haluz*** in the name of the national tradition. Later on Mises published an important history of modern philosophy in Hebrew.

Michael Pines, a writer in ***Ha-Lebanon***, and the opponent of Lilienblum, was the protagonist of the conservative party in Lithuania. His chief work, ***Yalde Ruhi*** ("The Children of My Spirit"), appeared in 1872 at Mayence. It may be considered the literary masterpiece on the conservative side, the counterstroke to Lilienblum's "Sins of Youth". It is a defense of traditional Judaism, and is instinct with an intuitive philosophy and with deep faith. Pines makes a closely reasoned claim for the right of the Jewish religion to exist in its integrity. Without being a fanatic, he believes, with Samuel David Luzzatto, that the religion of the Jew on its poetic side is the peculiar product of the Jewish national genius--that the religion, and not the artificial legal system engrafted upon it, is the essential part of Judaism. The ceremonies and the religious practices are necessary for the purpose of maintaining the harmony of the faith, "as the wick is necessary for the lamp". This harmony, reacting at once upon feeling and morality, cannot be undone by the results of science, and therefore the Jewish religion is eternal in its essence. The religious reforms introduced by the German Rabbis have but had the effect of drying up the springs of poetry in the religion, and as for the compromise between faith and life, extolled and urged by Lilienblum, it is only a futile phrase. Of what use is it, seeing that the religious feel no need of it, but on the contrary take delight in the religion as it stands, which fills the void in their soul?

Pines did not share the pessimistic fears of the realists of his time. A true conservative, he believed in the national rebirth of the people of Israel, and, a romantic

Jew, he dreamed of the realization of the humanitarian predictions of the prophets. Judaism to him is the pure idea of justice, "and every just idea ends by conquering the whole of humanity".

Extremes meet. There is one point in common between Lilienblum, the last of the humanists, the disillusioned skeptic, and Pines, the optimist of the ghetto. Both maintained that the action of the humanists was inefficacious, and the compromise between religion and life a vain expedient. Nevertheless, there was no possibility of bringing the two to stand upon the same platform. While the humanists, in abandoning the perennial dreams of the people, had separated themselves from its moral and religious life, and thus cut away the ground from under their own feet, the romantic conservatives paid no attention to the demands of modern life, the currents of which had loosed the foundations of the old world, and were threatening to carry away the last national breastwork.

A synthesis was needed to merge the two currents, the humanist and the romantic, and lead the languishing Haskalah back to the living sources of national Judaism. This was the task accomplished by Perez Smolenskin, the leader of the national progressive movement.

CHAPTER IX
THE NATIONAL PROGRESSIVE MOVEMENT
PEREZ SMOLENSKIN

Perez Smolenskin was born, in 1842, at Monastryshchina, a little market town near Mohilew. His father, a poor and an unfortunate man, who was not able to support his wife and six children successfully, was forced to leave his family on account of a slanderous accusation brought against him by a Polish priest. The mother, a plucky woman of the people, supported herself by hard work, in spite of which it was her ambition to make Rabbis of her boys. At length the father joined his family again, and a period of comparative prosperity set in.

The first care of the returned father was to look to the education of his two sons, Leon and Perez. The latter showed unusual ability. At the age of four he began the study of the Pentateuch, at five he had been introduced to the Talmud. These studies absorbed him until his eleventh year. Then, like all the sons of the ghetto desirous of an education, he left his father and mother, and betook himself to the *Yeshibah* at Shklow. The journey was made on foot, and his only escort was the blessing of his mother. The lad's youth proved no obstacle to his entering the Talmud academy, nor to his acquiring celebrity for industry and attainments. His brother Leon, who had preceded him to Shklow, initiated him in the Russian language, and supplied him with modern Hebrew writings. Openhearted and lively, he set prejudice at defiance, and maintained friendly relations with a certain intellectual who was reputed a heretic, an acquaintanceship that contributed greatly to the mental development of young Perez. The dignified burghers who were taking turns in supplying him with his meals, alarmed at his aberration from the straight path, one after another withdrew their protection from him. Black misery clutched him. He was but fourteen years old, and already he had entered upon a life of disquiet and adventure. His story is the Odyssey of an erring son of the ghetto. Repulsed by the **Mitnaggedim**, he sought help with the Hasidim. He was equally ill-fitted for their life. Their uncouth mystical exaltation, the absurdity of their superstitions, and their hypocrisy drove him to exasperation. He cast himself into the whirl of life, became assistant to a cantor at a synagogue, and then teacher of Hebrew and Talmud. The whole gamut of precarious employments open to a scholar of the ghetto he ran up and down again. His restless spirit and the desire to complete his education carried him to Odessa. There he established himself, and there years of work and endeavor were passed. He acquired the modern languages, his mind grew broader, and he gave up religious practices once for all, always remaining attached to Judaism, however.

In 1867 appeared his first literary production, the article against Letteris, who at that time occupied the position of an incontestable authority, in which Smolenskin permits himself to pass severe and independent criticism upon his Hebrew adaptation of Goethe's *Faust*. In the Odessa period falls also the writing of the first few chapters of his great novel, **Ha-To'eh be-Darke ha-Hayyim** ("A Wanderer Astray on the Path of Life"). [A complete edition of the novels and articles by Smolenskin appeared recently at St. Petersburg and Wilna, published by Katzenelenbogen.] But his free spirit could not adapt itself to the narrowness and meanness of the literary folk and the editors of periodicals. He determined to leave Russia for the civilized Occident, the promised land in the dreams of the Russian Maskilim, beautified by the presence of Rapoport and Luzzatto. His first destination was Prague, the residence of Rapoport, then Vienna, and later he pushed his way to Paris and London. Everywhere he studied and made notes. A sharp-eyed observer, he sought to probe European affairs as well as Occidental Judaism to their depths. He established relations with Rabbis, scholars, and Jewish notables, and finally he was in a position to appraise at close range the liberty he had heard vaunted so loudly, and the religious reforms wished for so eagerly by the intelligent of his own country. He soon had occasion to see the reverse of the medal, and his disenchantment was complete. Regretfully he came to the conclusion that the modern emancipation movement had brought the Jewish spirit in the Occident to the point at which the Western

Jew was turned away from the essence of Judaism. Form had taken the place of substance, ceremonial the place of religious and national sentiment. Heartsick over such disregard of the past, indignant at the indifference displayed by modern Jews toward all he held dear, young Smolenskin resolved to break the silence that was observed in the great capitals of Europe respecting all things Jewish and carry the gospel of the ghetto to the "neo-Gentiles".

The first shaft was delivered in Vienna, where he began the publication of his review *Ha-Shahar* ("Daybreak"). Almost without means, but fired by the wish to work for the national and moral elevation of his people, the young writer laid down the articles of his faith:

> "The purpose of *Ha-Shahar* is to shed the light of knowledge upon the paths of the sons of Jacob, to open the eyes of those who either have not beheld knowledge, or, beholding, have not understood in value, to regenerate the beauty of the Hebrew language, and increase the number of its devotees.
>
> "... But when the eyes of the blind begin to open slowly, and they shake off the sluggish slumber in which they have been sunk since many years, then there is still another class to be dealt with--those who, having tasted of the fruit of the tree of knowledge, intentionally close their eyes to our language, the only possession left to us that can bring together the hearts of Israel and make one nation of it all over the earth.... Let them take warning! If my hand is against the bigots and the hypocrites who hide themselves under the mantle of the truth, ... it will be equally unsparing of the enlightened hypocrites who seek with honeyed words to alienate the sons of Israel from their ancestral knowledge...."

War to mediaeval obscurantism, war to modern indifference, was the plan of his campaign. *Ha-Shahar* soon became the organ of all in the ghetto who thought, felt, and fought,--the spokesman of the nationalist Maskilim, setting forth their demands as culture bearers and patriots.

At a time when Hebrew literature consisted mainly of translations or works of minor significance, Smolenskin had the boldness to announce that the columns of his periodical would be open to writers of original articles only. The era of the translator and the vapid imitator had come to a close. A new school of original writers stepped upon the boards, and little by little the reading public accustomed itself to give preference to them.

And at a time when disparagement of the national element in Judaism had been carried to the furthest excess, Smolenskin asserted Judaism's right to exist, in such words as these:

> [The wilfully blind] "bid us to be like all the other nations, and I repeat after them: Let us be like all the other nations, pursuing and attaining knowledge, leaving off from wickedness and folly, and dwelling as loyal citizens in the lands whither we have been scattered. Yes, let us be like all the other nations, unashamed of the rock whence we have been hewn, like the rest in holding dear our language and the glory of our people. It is not a disgrace for us to believe that our exile will once come to an end, ... and we need not blush for clinging to the ancient language with which we wandered from people to people, in which our poets sang and our seers prophesied when we lived at ease in our own land, and in which our fathers poured out their hearts when their blood flowed like water in the sight of all.... They who thrust us away from the Hebrew language meditate evil against our people and against its glory!"

The reputation of ***Ha-Shahar*** was firmly established by the publication of Smolenskin's great novel ***Ha-To'eh be-Darke ha- Hayyim*** in its columns. In this as in the rest of his works, he is the prophet denouncing the crimes and the depravity of the ghetto, and proclaiming the revival of national dignity.

Smolenskin permitted himself to be thwarted by nothing in the execution of his bold designs, neither by the meagreness of his material resources nor by the animosities which his fearless course did not fail to arouse among literary men.

In 1872, Smolenskin published, at Vienna, his masterpiece *'Am 'Olam* ("The Eternal People"), which became the platform of the movement for national emancipation. Noteworthy from every point of view, this work shows him to have been an original thinker and an inspired poet, a humanist and at the same time a patriot. He is full of love for his people, and his faith in its future knows no limits. He demonstrates convincingly that true nationalism is not incompatible with the final realization of the ideal of the universal brotherhood of men. National devotion is but a higher aspect of devotion to family. In nature we see that, in the measure in which the individuality of a being is distinct, its superiority and its independence are increased. Differentiation is the law of progress. Why not apply the law to human groups, or nations?

The sum total of the qualities peculiar to the various nations, and the various ways in which they respond to concepts presented to them from without, these constitute the life and the culture of mankind as a whole. While admitting that the historical past of a people is an essential part of its existence, he believes it to be a still more urgent necessity for every people to possess a present ideal, and entertain national hopes for a better future. Judaism cherishes the Messianic ideal, which at bottom is nothing but the hope of its national rebirth. Unfortunately, the modern, unreligious Jew denies the ideal, and the orthodox Jew envelops it in the obscurity of mysticism.

The last chapter of "The Eternal People", called "The Hope of Israel", is pervaded by magnificent enthusiasm. For the first time in Hebrew, Messianism is detached from its religious element. For the first time, a Hebrew writer asserts that Messianism is the political and moral resurrection of Israel, **the return to the prophetic tradition**.

Why should the Greeks, the Roumanians, desire a national emancipation, and Israel, the people of the Bible, not?... The only obstacle is the fact that the Jews have lost the notion of their national unity and the feeling of their solidarity.

This conviction as to the existence of a Jewish nationality, the national emancipation dreamed by Salvador, Hess, and Luzzatto, considered a heresy by the orthodox and a dangerous theory by the liberals, had at last found its prophet. In Smolenskin's enthusiastic formulation of it, the ideal was carried to the masses in Russia and Galicia, superseding the mystical Messianism they had cherished before.

Smolenskin's combative spirit did not allow him to rest at that. The idea of national regeneration was in collision with the theory, raised to a commanding position by Mendelssohn and his school, that Judaism constitutes a religious confession. In a series of articles ("A Time to Plant, and a Time to Pluck up that which is Planted"), [***Ha- Shahar***, 1875-6.] he deals with the Mendelssohnian theory.

Proceeding from history and his knowledge of Judaism, he proves that the Jewish religion is not a rigid block of unalterable notions, but rather a body of ethical and philosophical teachings constantly undergoing a process of evolution, and changing its aspect according to the times and the environment. If this doctrine is the quintessence of the national genius of the Jew, it is nevertheless accessible, in theory and in practice, to whosoever desires access. It is not the dogmatic and exclusive privilege of a sacerdotal caste.

This is the rationale of Smolenskin's opposition to the religious dogmatism of Mendelssohn, who had wished to confine Judaism inside of the circle of Rabbinic law without recognizing its essentially evolutionary character. Maimonides himself is not spared by Smolenskin, for it was Maimonides who had set the seal of consecration upon logical dogmatism. The less does he spare the modern school of reformers. Religious reforms, he freely admits, are necessary, but they ought to be spontaneous developments, emanations from the heart of the believers themselves, in response to changes in the times and social relations. They ought not to be the artificial product of a few intellectuals who have long broken away from the masses of the people, sharing neither their suffering nor their hopes. If Luther succeeded, it was because he had faith himself. But the modern Jewish reformers are not believers, therefore their work does not abide. It is only the study of the Hebrew language, of the religion of the Jew, his culture, and his spirit that is capable of replacing the dead letter and soulless regulations by a keen national and religious sentiment in harmony with the exigencies of life. The next century, he predicted, would see a renewed, unified Judaism.

This is a summing up of the ideas which brought him approval and endorsement from all sides, but also, and to a greater degree, opposition and animosity, the latter from the old followers of the German humanist movement. One of them, the poet Gottlober, founded, in 1876, a rival review, ***Ha-Boker Or***, in which he pleaded the cause of the school of Mendelssohn. But the new periodical, which continued to appear until 1881, could neither supplant *Ha-Shahar*, nor diminish Smolenskin's ardor. Other obstacles of all sorts, and the difficulties raised by the Russian censor, were equally ineffectual in halting the efforts of the valiant apostle of Jewish nationalism. He was assured the cooperation of all independent literary men, for Smolenskin had never posed as a believer in dogmatic religion or as its defender. On the contrary, he waged constant war with Rabbinism. He was persuaded that an untrammelled propaganda, bold speech issuing from a knowledge of the heart of the masses and their urgent needs, would bring about a natural and peaceable revolution, restoring to the Jewish people its free spirit, its creative genius, and its lofty morality. It mattered little to him that the young had ceased to be orthodox: in case of need, national feeling would suffice to maintain Israel. At this point, it appears, Smolenskin excelled Samuel David Luzzatto and his school as a free-thinker. The Jewish people is to him the eternal people personifying the prophetic idea, realizable in the Jewish land and not in exile. The liberalism displayed by Europe toward the Jews during a part of the nineteenth century is in his opinion but a transient phenomenon, and as early as 1872 he foresaw the recrudescence of anti- Semitism.

This conception of Jewish life was welcomed by the educated as a revelation. The distinction of the editor of *Ha-Shahar* is that he knew how to develop the ideas enunciated by the masters preceding him, how to carry them to completion, and render them accessible to the people at large. He revealed a new formula to them, thanks to which their claims as Jews were no longer in contradiction with the demands of modern times. It was the revenge taken by the people speaking through the mouth of the writer. It was the echo of the cry of the throbbing soul of the ghetto.

CHAPTER X
THE CONTRIBUTORS TO HA-SHAHAR

Ha-Shahar soon became the centre of a hot crusade against obscurantism. The propaganda it carried on was all the more effectual as it opposed an out-of-date Judaism in the name of a national regeneration, the deathless ideal of the Jewish people. While admitting the principle that reforms are necessary, provided they are reasonable and slowly advanced, in agreement with the natural evolution of Judaism and not in opposition to its spirit, Smolenskin's review at the same time constituted itself the focus of a bold campaign against the kind of religious reform introduced by the moderns.

Whoever thought, felt, suffered, and was alive to the new ideas, hastened to range himself under the banner of the Hebrew review during its eighteen years of a more or less regular existence, the occasional interruptions being due to lack of funds. Its history forms an important chapter in that of Hebrew literature. Smolenskin possessed the art of stimulating well-tried powers, and discovering new talent and bringing it forward. The school of *Ha-Shahar* may almost be looked upon as the creation of his strong hand. Gordon, it is true, published the best of his satires in *Ha-Shahar*, and Lilienblum pursued his reform purposes in its columns, *'Olam ha-Tohu* ("The World of Chaos"), his ringing criticism of "The Hypocrite", being among the articles written by him for it, in which he casts upon Mapu's work the light of the utilitarian realism borrowed from the Russian writers of his time, and exposes it as a naive, unreal conception of Jewish life. Though these two veterans gave him their support, the larger number of the collaborators of Smolenskin made their first appearance in the world of letters under his auspices, and it was due to his influence that German and Austrian scholars returned to the use of Hebrew. On the other hand, the co-operation of eminent professors, such as Heller, David Muller, and others, contributed not a little to the success of **Ha-Shahar**.

The Galician novelist Mordecai D. Brandstatter is properly reckoned among the best of the contributors to the review. His novels, a collected edition of which appeared in 1891, are of distinguished literary interest. Brandstatter is the painter of the customs and manners of the Galician Hasidim, whom he rallies with kindliness that yet has a keen edge, and with perfect artistic taste. Almost he is the only humorist of the time. His style is classic without going to extremes. He often makes use of the Talmudic jargon peculiar to Rabbinical scholars, whom he has the skill to transfer to his canvas down to their slightest gestures and mannerisms. But he does not restrain his wit in showing up the ridiculous side of the moderns as well. His best-known novels, which have been translated into Russian and into German, are "Doctor Alfasi", "Mordecai Kisowitz", "The Beginning and the End of a Quarrel", etc. Brandstatter also wrote satires in verse. He has not a few points of resemblance to the painter of Galician Jewish manners in German, Karl Emil Franzos.

Solomon Mandelkern, the erudite author of a new Biblical Concordance, hailing from Dubno (1846-1902), was an inspired poet. His historical pieces, his satires, and his epigrams, published for the most part in **Ha-Shahar**, have finish and grace. In his Zionist poems, he gives evidence of an enlightened patriotism. His popularity he gained by a detailed history of Russia (**Dibre Yeme Russia**) in three volumes, published at Wilna, in 1876, and a number of other works, all written in a pure, Biblical style at once beautiful and lively.

Jehudah Lob Levin (born in 1845), surnamed Yehallel, another poet who was an habitual contributor to **Ha-Shahar**, owes his fame to the fervent realism of his poems, which, however, suffer from pompousness and prolixity. His first appearance in the review was with a collection of poems, **Sifte Renanot** ("The Lips of Song"), in 1867. A long, realistic poem of his, **Kishron ha-Ma'aseh** ("The Value of Work"), in which he extols the unrivalled place of work in the universe, also was published in **Ha-Shahar**. In this poem, as well as in his prose articles, he ranged himself with Lilienblum in demanding a reshaping of Jewish life on an utilitarian, practical basis.

The criticism of Jewish customs and manners was brilliantly done by M. Cahen and Ben-Zebi, to mention only two among the many journalists of talent. The "Letters from Mohilew" by the former testify to the impartiality and independence, not only of the author, but also of the editor who accepted them for his periodical. Ben-Zebi wrote "Letters from Palestine", in which he depicts the ways of the rapacious notables of the old school in his country.

Science, historical and philosophical, found a sure welcome in *Ha- Shahar*. Smolenskin knew how to arouse the interest of the educated in these branches, which had been neglected by writers of Hebrew in Russia. Besides such well-known names as Chwolson, the eminent professor, Harkavy, the indefatigable explorer of Jewish history in the Slav countries, and Gurland, the learned chronicler of the persecutions of the Jews in Poland, it is proper to make mention of David Kahana, one of the most eminent of the scientific contributors to *Ha-Shahar*, a scholar of distinction, who has succeeded in throwing light upon the obscure epoch of the false Messiahs and on the origin of Hasidism.

Dr. Solomon Rubin's ingenious philosophical studies on the origin of religions and the history of ancient peoples were also for the most part published in *Ha-Shahar*. Lazarus Schulman, the author of humorous tales, wrote a painstaking analysis of Heine for Smolenskin's periodical. Other contributors to the scientific department were Joshua Lewinsohn, Schorr, Jehiel Bernstein, Moses Ornstein, Dr. Kantor, and Dr. A. Poriess, the last of whom was the author of an excellent treatise on physiology in Hebrew. The productions of these writers did more for the spread of enlightenment than all the exhortations of the reformers.

Of litterateurs, the novelist Braudes, and the poets Menahem M. Dolitzki and Zebi Schereschewsky, etc., made their first appearance in the columns of *Ha-Shahar*.

The impetus issuing from *Ha-Shahar* was visible on all fields of Judaism. The number of Hebrew readers increased considerably, and the interest in Hebrew literature grew. The eminent scholar I. H. Weiss published his five-volume History of Tradition (*Dor Dor we- Doreshaw*) in Hebrew (Vienna, 1883-1890). Though it was a purely scientific work, laying bare the successive steps in the natural development of Rabbinic law, it produced a veritable revolution in the attitude of the orthodox of the backward countries.

As was mentioned above, Gottlober founded his review, *Ha-Boker Or*, in 1876, to ensure the continuity of the humanist tradition and defend the theories of the school of Mendelssohn. The last of the followers of German humanism rallied about it,--Braudes published his principal novel "Religion and Life" in it,--and it also attracted the last representatives of the *Melizah*, like Wechsler (*Ish Naomi*), who wrote Biblical criticism in an artificial, pompous style.

This artificiality, fostered in an earlier period by the *Melizim*, had by no means disappeared from Hebrew literature. Its most popular devotees in the later day of which we are speaking were, besides Kalman Schulman, A. Friedberg, who wrote a Hebrew adaptation of Grace Aguilar's tale, "The Vale of Cedars", published in 1876, and Ramesh, the translator of "Robinson Crusoe."

Translations continued to enjoy great vogue, and it was vain for Smolenskin, in the introduction to his novel *Ha-To'eh be-Darke ha- Hayyim*, to warn the public against the abuses of which translators were guilty. The readers of Hebrew sought, besides novels, chiefly works on the natural sciences and on mathematics, especially astronomy. Among the authors of original scientific books, Hirsch Rabinowitz should be given the first place, as the writer of a series of treatises on physics, chemistry, etc., which appeared at Wilna, between the years 1866 and 1880. After him come Lerner, Mises, Reifmann, and a number of others.

The period was also prolific in periodicals representing various tendencies. At Jerusalem appeared *Ha-Habazzelet*, *Sha'are Ziyyon* ("The Gates of Zion"), and others. On the American side of the Atlantic, the review *Ha-Zofeh be-Erez Nod* ("The Watchman in the Land of the Wanderer") reflected the fortunes and views of the educated among the immigrants in the New World. Even the orthodox had recourse to this modern expedient of periodicals in their endeavor to put up a defense of Rabbinism. The journal *Ha-Yareah* ("The Moon"), and particularly *Mahazike ha-Dat* ("The Pillars of the Faith"), both issued in Galicia, were the organs of the faithful in their opposition to humanism and progress. *Ha-Kol*, the journal founded by Rodkinson (1876-1880), with reform purposes, played a role of considerable importance in the conflict between the two parties.

Already tendencies were beginning to crop up radically different from any Judaism had betrayed previously. In 1877, when Smolenskin was publishing his weekly paper *Ha-Mabbit* ("The Observer"), Freiman founded the first Socialistic journal in Hebrew, *Ha-Emet* ("The Truth"). It also appeared in Vienna. And, again, S. A. Salkindson, a convert from Judaism, the author of admirable translations of "Othello" (1874) and "Romeo and Juliet" (1878), both published through the endeavors of Smolenskin, brought out the Hebrew translation of an epic wholly Christian in character, Milton's "Paradise Lost". It was a sign of the times that this work of art was enjoyed and appreciated by the educated Hebrew public in due accordance with its literary merits.

The clash of opinions and tendencies encouraged by the authority and the tolerance of Smolenskin was fruitful of results. *Ha-Shahar* had made itself the centre of a synthetic movement, progressive and national, which was gradually revealing the outline of its plan and aims. The reaction caused by the unexpected revival of anti-Semitism in Germany, Austria, Roumania, and Russia, had levelled the last ruins of German humanism in the West, and had put disillusionment in the place of dreams of equality in the East. Whoever remained faithful to the Hebrew language and to the ideal of the regeneration of the Jewish people, turned his eyes toward the stout-hearted writer who ten years earlier had predicted the overthrow of all humanitarian hopes, and had been the first to propose the practical solution of the Jewish problem by means of national reconstruction.

Smolenskin's fame had by this time transcended the circle of his readers and those interested in Hebrew literature. The **Alliance Israelite Universelle** entrusted to him the mission of investigating the conditions of the life of the Roumanian Jews. During his stay in Paris, Adolphe Cremieux, the tireless defender of the oppressed of his race, agreed, in conversation with him, that only those who know the Hebrew language, hold the key to the heart of the Jewish masses, and, Cremieux continued, he would give ten years of his life to have known Hebrew. [Brainin, in his admirable "Life of Smolenskin", Warsaw, 1897, p. 58; *Ha-Shahar*, X, 532.]

The war of 1877 between Russia and Turkey, and the nationalistic sentiments it engendered everywhere in Eastern Europe, awakened a patriotic movement among the Jewish youth who had until then resisted the idea of national emancipation. A young student in Paris, a native of Lithuania, Eliezer Ben-Jehudah, published two articles in *Ha- Shahar*, in 1878, in which, setting aside all religious notions, he urged the regeneration of the Jewish people on its ancient soil, and the cultivation of the Biblical language.

In 1880, Smolenskin, who had undertaken a new and complete edition of his works in twenty-four volumes, at Vienna, went on a tour through Russia. Great was his joy when he noted the results produced by his own activity, and saw that he had gained the affection and approval of all enlightened classes of Jews. Under the influence of **Ha-Shahar**, a new generation had grown up, free and nevertheless loyal to its nativity and to the ideal of Judaism. Smolenskin's journey resembled a triumphal procession. The university students at St. Petersburg and Moscow arranged meetings in honor of the Hebrew writer, at which he was acclaimed the master of the national tongue, the prophet of the rejuvenation of his people. In the provincial districts, similar scenes were enacted, and Smolenskin saw himself the object of honors never before accorded a Hebrew author. He returned to Vienna, encouraged to pursue the task he had assumed, and full of hope for the future.

It was the eve of the cataclysm foretold by the editor of **Ha- Shahar**.

CHAPTER XI
THE NOVELS OF SMOLENSKIN

Smolenskin owed his vast popularity and his influence on his contemporaries only in part to his work as a journalist. What brought him close to the people were his realistic novels, which occupy the highest place in modern Hebrew literature.

Smolenskin's first piece of fiction, ***Ha-Gemul*** ("The Recompense"), was published at Odessa, in 1868, on a subject connected with the Polish insurrection. Save its realistic style, there was nothing about it to betray the future novel writer of eminence.

It was said above, that Smolenskin wrote the early chapters of his ***Ha-To'eh*** while at Odessa, and, also, he planned another novel there, "The Joy of the Hypocrite". When he proposed working out the latter for publication in ***Ha-Meliz***, the editor rejected the idea disdainfully, saying that he preferred translations to original stories, so little likely did it seem that realistic writing could be done in Hebrew. Once he had his own organ, ***Ha-Shahar***, Smolenskin wrote and published novel after novel in it, beginning with his ***Ha-To'eh be-Darke ha-Hayyim***. In ***Ha-Shahar*** it appeared in three parts. Later it came out in book form, in four volumes. It is the first work of the Hebrew realistic school worthy of being classed as such.

As Cervantes makes his hero Don Quixote pass through all the social strata of his time, so the Hebrew novelist conducts his wanderer, Joseph the orphan, through the nooks and corners of the ghetto. He introduces him to all the scenes of Jewish life, he displays before his eyes all its customs and manners, he makes him a witness to all its superstitions, fanaticism, and sordidness of every kind, a physical and social abasement that has no parallel. A faithful observer, an impressionist, an unemphatic realist, he discloses on every page misunderstood lives, extravagant beliefs, movements, evils, greatnesses, and miseries, of which the civilized world had not the slightest suspicion. It is the Odyssey of the ghetto adventurer, the life and journeyings of the author himself, magnified, and enveloped in the fictitious circumstances in which the hero is placed, a human document of the greatest significance.

Joseph, the orphan, whose father, persecuted by the Hasidim, disappeared, and whose mother died in abject misery, is received into the house of his uncle, the same brother of his father who had caused the father's ruin. Abused by a wicked aunt and driven by an irresistible hankering after a vagabond life, he runs away from his foster home. First he is picked up by a band of rascally mendicants, then he becomes an inmate in the house of a **Baal-Shem**, a charlatan wonder-worker, and thus a changeful existence leads him to traverse the greater part of Jewish Russia. In a series of photographic pictures, Smolenskin reproduces in detail the ways and exploits of all the bohemians of the ghetto, from the beggars up to the peripatetic cantors, their moral shortcomings, their spitefulness, and their insolence. Impelled by the wish to acquire an education, and perhaps also put a roof over his head, Joseph finally enters a celebrated **Yeshibah**. It is the salvation of the young tramp. He is given food, he sleeps on the school benches, and he is rescued from military service. But soon, having incurred disfavor by his frankness, and especially because he is discovered reading secular books, in which he is initiated by one of his fellow-students, he is obliged to leave the Yeshibah. By the skin of his teeth he escapes being packed off to the army as a soldier. He takes refuge with the Hasidim, and has the good fortune to find favor in the eyes of the **Zaddik** ("Saint") himself.

But very soon he revolts against the equivocal transports of the saintly sect. In his wanderings, Joseph doubtless meets with good people, disinterested idealists, simple men and women of the rank and file, Rabbis worthy of the highest praise, enthusiastic intellectuals, but the ordinary life of the ghetto, abnormal and narrow, disgusts him completely. He departs to seek a freer life in the West. Passing through Germany without stopping, he goes on to London. Everywhere he makes Jewish society the object of study, and everywhere he suffers disillusionment. **Ha-To'eh** is a veritable encyclopedia of Jewish life at the beginning of the second half of the nineteenth century.

As a work of fiction, the novel cannot bear inspection. It is a succession of fantastic, sometimes incoherent events, an artificial complex of personages appearing on the scene at the will of the author, and acting like puppets on wires. The miraculous abounds, and the characters are in part exaggerated, in part blurred.

On the other hand, it is an incomparable work taken as a panorama of realistic scenes, not always consecutive scenes, but always absolutely true to life--a gallery of pictures of the ghetto.

Joseph is a painter, a realist first and last, and an impressionist besides. Looking at the lights and shadows of his picture, we feel that what we see is not all pure, spontaneous art. Like Auerbach and like Dickens, he is a thinker, a teacher. A true son of the ghetto, he preaches and moralizes. Sometimes he goes too far in his desire to impress a lesson. The reader perceives too clearly that the author has not remained an indifferent outsider while writing his novel. It is evident that his heart is torn by contradictory emotions--pity, compassion, scorn, anger, and love, all at once.

In point of style also the novel is a realistic piece of work. Smolenskin does not resort to Talmudisms, like Gordon and Abramowitsch, but, also, he takes care not to indulge in too many Biblical metaphors. This sometimes necessitates circumlocutions, and on the whole his oratorical manner leads to prolixity, but his prose always remains pure, flowing, and precise in the highest degree.

To illustrate Smolenskin's way of writing, and all the peculiarity of the social life he depicts, we cannot do better than translate a few passages from his novel dealing with characteristic phases of ghetto life.

Joseph is narrating his adventures and the impressions of his daily routine. The following is his striking description of the *Heder*, the well-known primary school of the ghetto, when his uncle first enters him there as a pupil:

"When I say house, let not the reader imagine a stone structure. What he would see is a small, low building, somewhat like a dog's kennel, built of thin boards, rotten at that. The thatch that covers it by way of roof hangs down to the ground, and yet it cannot keep off the rain, for the goats browsing in the neighborhood have munched off half of it to satisfy their appetite. Within there is a single room covered with black soot, the four walls garnished with spider-webs, and the floor paved with mortar. On the eastern wall hangs a large sheet of paper with the inscription, 'Hence blows the breath of life', which not many visitors will believe, because, instead of a quickening breath, pestilential odors enter by the window and offend the nostrils of those whose olfactory nerve has not lost all sensitiveness.... On the opposite wall, to the west, appear the words, 'A memorial unto the destruction of the Temple'. To this day I do not know what there was to commemorate the fall of the Holy Place. The rickety rafters? Or were the little creatures swarming all over the walls to remind one of 'the foxes that walk upon the mountain of Zion'?

"A huge stove occupies one-fourth of the room-space. Between the stove and the wall, to the right, is a bed made up ready for use, and on the other side a smaller one full of straw and hay, and without bed-covers. Opposite to it stands a large deal table tattoed with marks that are the handiwork of the **Melammed**. With his little penknife, which was never out of his hands, he would cut them into the wood all the time he was teaching us-- figures of beasts and fowl, and queer words....

"Around this table about ten boys were sitting, some conning the Talmud and others the Bible. One of the latter, seated at the right of the teacher, was reading aloud, in a sing-song voice, the section of the Pentateuch assigned for the following Sabbath in the synagogue, and his cantillation blended with the crooning of the teacher's wife as she sat by her baby's bed, ... but every now and then the master's voice rose and drowned the sounds of both, as the growl of the thunder stifles the roar of the waves.

"... The teacher was hideous to behold. He was short of stature and thin, his cheeks were withered looking, his nose long and

aquiline. His two ***Peot*** [1] were raven black and hung down like ropes by the side of his face. Old as he was, his cheeks showed only tufts of beard here and there, on account of his habit of plucking the hairs out one by one when he was absorbed in thought, not to mention those plucked out by his wife without the excuse of thinking. His black cap shone like a buttered roll, his linen shirt was neither an Egyptian nor a Swiss fabric, and his chest, overgrown with long black hair, always showed bare through the slit of his unbuttoned shirt. His linen trousers had been white once upon a time, but now they were picturesquely variegated from the dust and soot clinging to them, and by the stains added by his young hopeful, when he sat and played on his knees, by way of contributing his share to the glory in which his father was resplendently arrayed.... His ***Zizzit*** hung down to his bare feet. When my uncle entered the house, the teacher jumped up and ran hither and thither, seeking his shoes, but he could not find them. My uncle relieved him from his embarrassment by presenting me, with the words, 'Here is a new pupil for you!' Calming down, the teacher resumed his seat, and when we approached him, he tapped me on my cheek, saying, 'What hast thou learnt, my son?' All the pupils opened their mouth and eyes in amazement, and looked at me with envy. These many days, since they themselves were entered as new pupils in the school, they had not heard such gentle words issue from the mouth of the teacher...."
[1: See Lev. XIX, 27.]

This odd school prepared the child of the ghetto in very deed for the life and the struggle for existence awaiting him. In the next higher school, the Yeshibah, the ***alma mater*** of the Rabbinical student, the happenings were no less curious.

The young people in those strange colleges, for the most part precocious urchins, fall into classes, which, however, are not sharply divided off from one another. Day and night they sit bent over the huge folios of the Rabbis, occupied constantly with the study of the Law. Their meals are furnished them by the humble people of the town, often under deplorable conditions, and, on the whole, the life they lead is misery not untinged with humiliation. Such are the student years of the future Rabbis. And yet this bohemian existence is not destitute of picturesque elements and attractive features. Frequently it is at the Yeshibah that the young man for the first time finds sincere friends for whom he forms a lasting attachment, and they become his trusted advisers. It is a mob of young people, enthusiastic and impetuous, yet among them is found the aristocracy of the ghetto, those endowed with extraordinary intellectual gifts, and the devotion displayed by some of them to Talmudic knowledge is absolutely sublime.

Smolenskin paints a characteristic Yeshibah scene enacted by these embryonic Talmudists:

"It is a strange spectacle that meets the eye of the observer on his first visit to the women's gallery in the Yeshibah [at nightfall]. He finds it suddenly transformed into a gathering-place for merchants. The boys who have bread or money, try their hands at trafficking, and those who have neither bread nor money, try theirs at theft, and a large group of those who loathe the one pursuit as well as the other, sit apart and entertain each other with the wonderful exploits of brigands, and giants, and witches, and devils, and evil spirits, who are abroad at night to affright human beings, and the dead who leave their graves to terrify the wicked or cure the sick with grass of the field, and many more such tales that delight the heart and soul of the listeners. Such things have I myself seen even while the afternoon and the evening prayers were going on below. I heard confused sounds. One would cry out, 'Who wants bread?' And another would sing out in reply, 'Who has bread to sell? Who has bread to sell?'--'Here is bread!'--'Will you take a penny for it?'--'Two pennies, and no less!'--'Some one has stolen my bread! Who stole my bread?'--' My bread is first-class! Come and buy!'--'But I haven't a red copper!'--'All right, give me a pledge!'--

'You may have my troubles as a pledge, you old curmudgeon!'--'Here are two pennies, give me the bread!'--'Get out, I was ahead of you!'--'I insist upon my rights, I was the first.'--'Why, I handed my money over long ago, it is my bread.'--'You stole my bread.'--'You lie, it's my bread!'--'You're a liar, a thief, a robber!'--'The devil take you, you hound!'--'Wait a moment, and I'll show you my teeth, if I'm a hound!'

"And so the words fly from mouth to mouth in the women's gallery, and cuffs and blows are not rare things, either, and not one of the boys remembers that the congregation below is at prayers. They go on trafficking and telling tales undisturbed, until the end of the service, and then they return to their seats, every boy to his own at the long tables, which are lighted each of them by a single candle for its whole length. A dispute breaks out as to where the candle is to stand. First one draws it up to himself, and then another wrests it from his hand and sets it next to his own book, and finally all decide to measure the table. One of the boys takes off his belt, and ascertains the breadth of the table and its length, and the candle is put in the exact centre. The quarrel is settled, and the students begin to drawl the text before them, and what they did the whole livelong day, they continue to do at night.

"Then one of them says, 'I sold my bread for two pennies'.--'And I bought an apple for one penny and a cake for half a penny', returns another.--'Darkness swallow up the monitor! He doesn't give us enough candles to light up the dark!'--'The devil take him!'--'A plague on him!'--'I am going on a visit home at Passover.'--'Sarah the widow lent me three pennies.'

"While the boys talk thus over their open books, their bodies are swaying to and fro like reeds in a pond, and their voices rise and fall in the same sing-song in which they con their texts, all to deceive the monitor, who, hearing the usual drawl and seeing the rocking bodies, believes the students to be busy at their tasks. But little by little, they forget and drop out of their recitative into the ordinary conversational tone.--'Tell me, Zabualean [the pupils are called by their native town in the Yeshibah], don't you think it's about time for the angel of death to come and carry off our monitor? Or is he going to live forever?'--'I pray to God to afflict his body with such ills that he cannot come to the Yeshibah. Then we should have rest. I take good care not to ask for his death. Another would take his place, and there's no telling whether he would not be worse. If pain keeps him abed, we shall have a respite.'--'But aren't you committing a sin, cursing a deaf man?' interposes one of the boys, indignantly.--'Look at that Azubian! A saint, isn't he? Proof enough that he has seven sins hidden in his heart!' retorts the Zabualean.--'No need of any such proof! Why, this very Azubian could not resist the tempter, and is hard at work studying Russian. That's as bad as bad can be, you don't have to search out hidden sins.'--'I at least am not perverting the right,' the Azubian flings out, 'because the Talmud itself says that the law of the land is law, but you are committing an actual sin against the Torah in cursing....' The sentence was never finished, for the monitor had been standing behind the table observing the boys for some time, and when he saw the excitement of the Azubian,--being deaf, he could not hear what he said,--he threw himself upon him, and, seizing him by the ear, shook him as violently as his strength permitted, crying, 'You wretches, you rebels, there, that's for you!' and he beat another boy with his fists, and struck a third upon his cheeks.--'The monitor has rained profuse kisses upon the Azubian for defending him!' one of the boys paraphrased Proverbs, [1] drawling in the approved sing-song, and keeping his eyes fixed upon his book. The others burst into loud laughter at the sally. Even those who were still smarting from the monitor's blows could not restrain themselves and joined in. 'Are you making fun of me? You're not afraid?' thundered the monitor, in towering rage, turning this way and that, uncertain whom to select as the first victim of his heavy hand. Before he could collect his wits, one of the boys yelled, 'Rabbi Isaac, Rabbi Isaac, the candles!'--It worked like a conjurer's charm upon a serpent. In an instant the monitor turned and ran to his room and searched it. Seeing no one there, he sank into his chair, and groaned: 'Wicked, depraved children! Those gallows-birds, I'll mangle their flesh, and flay the skin from their bones!' and he kept on mumbling to himself in this strain, until sleep fell upon his eyelids shaded by long eyebrows white as snow, and his head dropped into his hands resting upon the table.

"As soon as he slept, the boys resumed their talk, and my friend continued to tell me about life in the Yeshibah.... 'Do you think that the Yeshibah students are guileless youths who have never dropped their mother's apron strings? If you do, you are vastly mistaken. They are up to all the tricks, and the dullest among them can show a thing or two to the best of the rich boys. You will do well to observe their ways and learn from them.'--'I shall try to walk in their footsteps.'....

"Then I went out to get my supper. On returning I found the greater part of the boys had gone to sleep, and almost all the candles were out. Only a few of the students were sitting together and talking. I sought out my friend, and discovered him lying upon one of the tables in the women's gallery, but he was still awake. 'Why don't you look for a place to lie down in?' he asked me.--'I shall lie here next to you,' I replied.--' No, you can't do that. Here each boy has a place in which he always sleeps; he never changes about. Go down to the men's hall and look for an unoccupied spot. If you find a table, so much the better. If not, you must be satisfied with a bench.'--I did as he advised. I found a long table in the men's hall, but hardly was I stretched out upon it when a boy took me by the scruff of my neck and shook me, saying: 'Get out, this is my place! And all the tables here are taken by boys who came to the Yeshibah long ahead of you. You must look for another place.'

"Not very much pleased, I slipped down from the table, and lay on the bench. But I could not go to sleep. I was not accustomed to the narrow board, nor to sleep without a bed-cover, and the little and big insects that swarmed in the cracks of the wood came forth from their nests and tickled me all over my body. But there was nothing to do, and I lay there in discomfort until all the lights were extinguished. Only one light of all burnt the whole night, the ***Ner tamid***, and under it sat two students, the 'watchers' [whose duty it was to continue at their task until morning, so that the study of the Law might not be interrupted day or night]."
[1: XXVII, 6.]

A life full of excitement, of which the above is a specimen, was not likely to displease so adventurous a spirit as Joseph's. When all is said, the Yeshibah provided a living for the young people, not overabundant, it is true, but at least they were relieved of material cares. The pious middle class Jews, and even the poor, considered it their duty to supply the needs of the young Talmudists, and the ambition of the latter was satisfied by the general good feeling that prevailed in their favor. For the aristocracy among the Jews, whose minds had not yet been stimulated by the new ideas, the Yeshibah was the home of all the virtues, the school in which the ideal was pursued, and lofty dreams were dreamed.

In another novel, "The Joy of the Hypocrite," which appeared in Vienna, in 1872, Smolenskin extols the idealism of his hero Simon, a product of the Yeshibah:

"Who had implanted in the mind of Simon the ideal of justice and the sublime word? Who had kindled in his soul the sacred flame, love of truth and research? Verily, he had found all these in the Yeshibah. Glory and increase be to you, ye holy places, last refuges of Israel's real heritage! From your portals came forth the elect destined from birth to be the light of their people and breathe new life into the dry bones."

Even during the period of the ***Behalah*** ("Terror") the Yeshibah remained unscathed, beyond the reach of misery and baseness. The venal jobbers, who, with the assistance of the Kahal, delivered the sons of the poor to the army in order to shield the rich, did not dare invade the Rabbinical schools. Like the Temple in ancient times, the ***Yeshibot*** offered a sure refuge. Whenever these sanctuaries were imperilled, national sentiment was aroused, and the threatened encroachments upon the last national treasure were resisted with bitter determination, for the idealism of the people of the ghetto, their hope and their faith, were enshrined there.

Joseph forfeited the privilege of sanctuary residing in the Yeshibah on the day he was taken redhanded, in the act of reading a profane book. Religious fanaticism had never proceeded with so much rigor as during the reign of terror following upon the disorganization of the social life of the Jews by the authorities, and the triumphant assertion of arbitrary power. Nevertheless, even at this disheartening juncture, the Rabbinical schools were the asylum of whatever of ideal or sublime there remained in Israel.

They furnished all the champions of humanism and the preachers and disseminators of civilization. In them Joseph met the generous comrades who introduced him to the Haskalah, and awakened love for the noble and the good in him, and boundless devotion to his people.

Hard as flint toward the inefficient leaders, without pity for the hypocrites and the fanatics, the heart of Joseph yet pulsated with love for the Jewish masses. Their unsympathetic surroundings and the persecutions to which they were exposed but increased his compassion for the straying flock of his people. In the general degradation, he succeeded in rising to moral heights, and so could set himself up for an impartial judge. He did not permit himself to be carried away by the sadness of the moment, though he did not remain indifferent to it, and his heart bled at the thought of his people's sufferings. In the human desert, in which he delighted to disport himself, he discovered noble characters, lofty sentiments, generous friendships, and, above all, lives devoted entirely to the pursuit of the ideal undeterred by any obstacle.

One after the other he presents the idealists of the ghetto to the reader. There is, first of all, Jedidiah, the common type of the Maskil, working zealously for culture, spreading truth and light in all the circles he can reach, dreaming of a Judaism, just, enlightened, exalted. Then there are the ardent young apostles, like that noble friend of Joseph, Gideon, most enlightened and most tolerant of Maskilim. In the measure in which Gideon detests fanaticism, he loves the people. He loves the masses with the heart of a patriot and the soul of a prophet. He loves them exactly as they are, with their beliefs, their simple faith, their poor, submissive lives, their ambitions as the chosen people, and their Messianic hope, to which he himself clings, though in a way less mystical than theirs. Thrilling, patriotic exaltation pervades the chapter on "The Day of Atonement." There Smolenskin appears as a genuine romanticist.

* * * * *

Such in outline are the features of this chaotic, superb novel, which, in spite of its faults of technique, remains to this day the truest and the most beautiful product of neo-Hebrew literature.

Ten years after finishing it, the author added a fourth part, which, on the whole, is nothing but an artificial collection of letters relating only indirectly to the main story. Joseph takes us with him through the Western lands, and then to Russia, whither he returns. In France and in England, he deplores the degeneracy of Judaism, attributing it to the ascendency of the Mendelssohnian school, and he foresees the approach of anti-Semitism. In Russia, he notes the prevalence of economic misery in frightful proportions, especially in the small rural towns, while in the large centres he regrets to see that the communities use every effort to imitate Occidental Judaism with all its faults. The overhasty culture of the Russian Jews, weakly correlated with the economic and political conditions under which they lived, was bound to bring on the breaking up of the passive idealism which constituted their chief strength.

The novel **Keburat Hamor** ("The Burial of the Ass") is the most elaborate and the most finished of Smolenskin's works. It describes the time of the "Terror" and the domination of the Kahal. The hero, Hayyim Jacob, is a wag, but pleasantries are not always understood in the ghetto, and he is made to pay for them. His practical jokes and his small respect for the notables of the community, whom he dares to defy and poke fun at, are his ruin.

He was scarcely more than a child when he was guilty of unprecedented conduct. Wrapped in blue drapery, like a corpse risen from the grave, and spreading terror wherever he appeared, he made his way one evening into the room in which cakes were stored for the next day's annual banquet of the **Hebrah Kadisha** ("Holy Brotherhood"), the all-powerful society, organized primarily to perform the last rites and ceremonies for the dead, to which the best Jews of a town belong. He got possession of all the dainty morsels, and made away with them. It was an unpardonable crime, high treason against saintliness. An inquiry was ordered, but the culprit was not discovered.

In revenge, the Brotherhood ordained the "burial of an ass" for the nameless criminal, and the verdict was recorded in the minutes of the society.

The incorrigible Hayyim Jacob continues to perpetrate jokes, and the Kahal decides to surrender him to the army recruiting officer. Warned betimes, he is able to make good his escape. He returns to his native town later on under an assumed name, imposes upon everybody by his scholarship, and marries the daughter of the head of the community. But his natural inclinations get the upper hand again. Meantime, he has confided the tale of his youthful tricks to his wife. She is disturbed by what she knows, she cannot endure the idea of the unparalleled punishment that awaits her husband should he be identified, for to undergo the "burial of an ass" is the supremest indignity that can be offered to a Jew. The body of the offender is dragged along the ground to the cemetery, and there it is thrown into a ditch made for the purpose behind the wall enclosing the grounds. But was not her father the head of the community? Could he not annul the verdict? She discloses the secret to him, and the effect is to fill him with instantaneous rage: What! to that wicked fellow he has given his daughter, to that heretic! He wants to force him to give up his wife, but no more than the husband will the woman listen to any such proposal. Hayyim Jacob succeeds in ingratiating himself with his father-in-law, though by fraud and only for a short time. After that, one persecution after another is inflicted upon him, and he succumbs.

So much for the background upon which the novelist has painted his scenes, authentic reproductions from the life of the Jews in Russia. The character of Hayyim Jacob stands out clear and forceful. His wife Esther is the typical Jewish woman, loyal and devoted unto death, of irreproachable conduct under reverses of fortune, and braving a world for love of her husband. The prominent characters of the ghetto are drawn with fidelity, though the colors are sometimes laid on too thick. The author has been particularly happy in re-creating the atmosphere of the ghetto, with its contradictions and its passions, the specialized intellectuality which long seclusion has forged for it, and its odd, original conception of life.

Smolenskin goes to the Yeshibah for the subject of one of his novels, **Gemul Yesharim** ("The Recompense of the Righteous"). The author describes the part played by the Jewish youth in the Polish insurrection. The ingratitude of the Poles proves that the Jews have nothing to expect from others, and they should count only upon their own resources.

Gaon we-Sheber ("Greatness and Ruin") is a collection of scattered novelettes, some of which are veritable works of art.

Ha-Yerushah ("The Inheritance") is the last of Smolenskin's great novels. It was first published in **Ha-Shahar**, in 1880-81. Its three volumes are full of incoherencies and long drawn out arguments. The life of the Jews of Odessa, however, and of Roumania, is well depicted, and also the psychologic stages through which the older humanists pass, deceived in their hopes, and groping for a return to national Judaism.

Smolenskin's last novel, **Nekam Berit** ("Holy Vengeance", **Ha-Shahar**, 1884), is wholly Zionistic. It was the author's swan song. Not long after its completion, an illness carried him off.

* * * * *

The novels of Smolenskin are a series of social documents and propagandist writings rather than works of pure art. Their chief defects are the incoherence of the action, the artificiality of the ***denouement***, their simplicity in all that concerns modern life, as well as their excessive didactic tendencies and the long-winded style of the author. Most of these defects he shares with such writers as Auerbach, Jokai, and Thackeray, with whom he may be placed in the same class. In passing judgment, it must be borne in mind that the Hebrew writer's life was one prolonged and bitter struggle for bare existence, his own and ***Ha-Shahar's***, for the periodical never yielded him any income. Only his idealism and the consciousness of the useful purpose he was serving sustained him in critical moments. These circumstances explain why his works bear the marks of hasty production. However that may be, since he gave them to the Jewish world, his novels have, even more than his articles, exercised unparalleled influence upon his readers.

In a word, the life of the Russian ghetto, its misery and its passions, the positive and the negative types of that vanishing world, have been set down in the writings of Smolenskin with such power of realism and such profound knowledge of conditions that it is impossible to form a just idea of Russo-Polish Judaism without having read what he has written.

CHAPTER XII
CONTEMPORANEOUS LITERATURE

The years 1881-1882 mark off a distinct era in the history of the Jewish people. The revival of anti-Semitism in Germany, the unexpected renewal of persecutions and massacres in Russia and Roumania, the outlawing of millions of human beings, whose situation grew less tenable from day to day in those two countries--such were the occurrences that disconcerted the most optimistic.

In the face of the precipitate exodus of crazed masses of the people and the urgency of decisive action, the old disputes between humanists and nationalists were laid aside. There could be but one choice between impossible assimilation with the Slav people on the one hand, and the idea, on the other hand, of a national emancipation divested of its mystical envelope and supplied with a territory as a practicable basis. All the Hebrew-writing authors were agreed that the time had passed for wrangling over a divergence of opinions. It was imperative that all forces should range themselves on the side of action. Even a skeptic like Gordon issued at that time, among many things like it, his thrilling poem: "We were a people, and we will a people be--with our young and with our old will we go!"

But whither? Some decided for America with the Western philanthropists, others, with Smolenskin, declared absolutely in favor of Palestine, the country of the Jew's perennial dreams.

Academic discussions of such questions are futile. It may safely be left to time and experience to decide between the two currents of opinion. As early as 1880, the young dreamer Ben-Jehudah, inspired with the idea of reviving the Hebrew as a national language, left Paris and established himself at Jerusalem. And from Lithuania came the romantic conservative Pines, forsaking the distinguished position he occupied there, in order to give his aid in the elevation of the Jews of Palestine. The tracks made by these two pioneers issuing from opposite camps were soon trodden by the followers of important movements.

A select circle of four hundred university students, indignant at the humiliating position into which they had been forced, thundered forth an appeal that resounded throughout the length and breadth of Jewish Russia: **Bet Ya'akob, leku we-nelekah** ("O House of Jacob, come ye and let us walk"). The practical result was the organization of the group BILU, the first to leave for Palestine and establish a colony there. [Is. II, 5. BILU are the initials of the four words of the Hebrew sentence quoted above.] This nucleus was enlarged by the accession of hundreds of middle class burghers and of the educated, and thus Jewish colonization was a permanently assured fact in the Holy Land.

The surprising return of the younger generation, who had wholly broken with Judaism, this first step toward the actual realization of the Zionist dream, has had most important consequences for the renascence of Hebrew literature. As for the educated element that had never, at least in spirit, left the ghetto, men like Lilienblum, Braudes, and others, whose later activity, a propaganda for economic reforms and instruction in manual trades, had almost ceased to have a reason for continuing,--as for them, their adhesion to Zionism could not be long delayed. And even outside of the ghetto a voice was heard, the authoritative voice of Dr. Leon Pinsker, announcing his support of the philo-Palestinian movement, as it was then called. In his brochure "Auto-Emancipation", the learned physician of Odessa, one of the old guard of staunch humanists, declares that the disease of anti-Semitism is a chronic affection, incurable as long as the Jews are in exile. There is but one solution for the Jewish question, the national regeneration of the Jews upon their ancient soil.

A new dawn began to break upon the horizon of the Jewish people. Hebrew literature was stimulated as never before, and the enthusiasm of the writers incorporated itself in the spirited proposals of Moses Eismann, Professor Schapira, and a number of others. In this sudden blossoming of patriotic ideas, excesses were inevitable. A chauvinistic reaction was not long in setting in. The religious reformers were attacked, they were accused of hindering a fusion of diverse parties in Judaism whose cordial agreement was indispensable to the success of the new movement.

Smolenskin alone was irreproachable. He who had never acknowledged the benefits of assimilation, had no need now to go to extremes. He remained faithful to his patriotic ideal, without renouncing any of his humanitarian and cultural aspirations. The activity he displayed was feverish. Now that he no longer stood alone in the defense of his ideas, he redoubled his efforts with admirable energy--encouraging here, exhorting there. But he was coming to the end of his strength, exhausted by a life of struggle and wretchedness, by long overtaxing of his physical and mental powers. He died in 1885, in the vigor of his years, cut off by disease. The whole of Jewry mourned at his grave. And *Ha- Shahar* soon ceased to exist.

* * * * *

With the extinction of *Ha-Shahar* we arrive at the end of the task we have set ourselves, of following up a phase of literary evolution. Modern Hebrew literature, for a century the handmaiden of one preponderating idea, the humanist idea in all its various applications, henceforth enters upon a new phase of its development. Led back by Smolenskin to its national source, stripped of every religious element, and imposed by the force of circumstances upon the masses and the educated alike, as the link uniting them thenceforth for the furtherance of the same patriotic end, it has again taken its place as the language of the Jewish people. It has ceased to serve as the mere mediator between Rabbinism and modern life. It is become an end in itself, an important factor in the life of the Jews. It is no longer a parasite flourishing at the expense of orthodoxy, from which it has for a century been luring away successive generations of the best of the young men, who, however, once emancipated, hastened to abandon that to which they owed their enlightenment. It has become the receptacle of the national literature of the Jewish people.

In 1885, when the distinguished editor of *Ha-Zefirah*, Nahum Sokolow, undertook the publication of the great literary annual, *He- Asif* ("The Collector"), the success he achieved went beyond the wildest expectations. The edition ran up to seven thousand copies. It was followed by other enterprises of a similar character, notably *Keneset Yisrael* ("The Assembly of Israel"), published by Saul Phinehas Rabbinowitz, the learned historian.

The Renascence of Hebrew Literature (1743-1885)

In 1886, the journalist, Jehudah Lob Kantor, encouraged by the vogue acquired by the Hebrew language, founded the first daily paper in it, ***Ha-Yom*** ("The Day"), at St. Petersburg. The success of this organ induced ***Ha-Meliz*** and ***Ha-Zefirah*** to change into dailies. A Hebrew political press thus came into being, and it has contributed tremendously to the spread of Zionism and culture. Even the Hasidim, who had until then remained contumacious toward modern ideas, were reached by its influence. It was, however, the Hebrew language that profited most by the development of journalism in it. The demands of daily life enriched its vocabulary and its resources, completing the work of modernization.

In Palestine, the need felt for an academic language common to the children of immigrants from all countries was a great factor in the practical rehabilitation of Hebrew as the vernacular. Ben-Jehudah was the first to use it in his home, in intercourse with the members of his family and his household, and a number of educated Jews followed his example, not permitting any other to be spoken within their four walls. In the schools at Jerusalem and in the newly-established colonies, it has become the official language. A recoil from the Palestinian movement was felt in Europe and in America, and a limited number of circles were formed everywhere in which only Hebrew was spoken. The journal ***Ha- Zebi*** ("The Deer"), published by Ben-Jehudah, became the organ of Hebrew as a spoken language, which differs from the literary language only in the greater freedom granted it of borrowing modern words and expressions from the Arabic and even from the European languages, and by its tendency to create new words from old Hebrew roots, in compliance with forms occurring in the Bible and the Mishnah. Here are a couple of examples of this tendency: The Hebrew word ***Sha'ah*** means "time", "hour". To this word the modern Hebrew adds the termination ***on***, making it ***Sha'on***, with the meaning "watch", or "clock". The verb ***darak***, in Biblical Hebrew "to walk", gives rise in the modern language to ***Midrakah***, "pavement."

The spread of the language and the increase in the number of readers together produced a change in the material condition of the writers. Their compensation became ampler in proportion, the consequence of which was that they could devote themselves to work requiring more sustained effort, and what they produced was more finished in detail. With the founding of the publishing society ***Ahiasaf***, and more particularly the one called ***Tushiyah***, due to the energy of Abraham L. Ben-

Avigdor, a sympathetic writer, Hebrew was afforded the possibility of developing naturally, in the manner of a modern language.

There was a short interval of non-production, caused by the brutality and sadness of unexpected events, but literary creativeness recovered quickly, and manifested itself, with growing force, in varied and widespread activity worthy of a literature that had grown out of the needs of a national group. On the field of poetry, there is, first of all, Constantin Shapiro, the virile lyricist, who knew how to put into fitting words the indignation and revolt of the people against the injustice levelled against them. His "Poems of Jeshurun" published in ***He-Asif*** for 1888, alive with emotion and patriotic ardor, as well as his Haggadic legends, must be put in the first rank. After him comes Menahem M. Dolitzki, the elegiac poet of Zionism, the singer of sweet "Zionides." [Poems published in New York, in 1896.] Then a young writer, snatched away all too early, Mordecai Zebi Manne, who was distinguished for his tender lyrics and deep feeling for nature and art. [His works appeared in Warsaw in 1897.] And, finally, there is Naphtali Herz Imber, the song-writer of the Palestinian colonies, the poet of the reborn Holy Land and the Zionist hope. [Poems published at Jerusalem in 1886.]

Among the latest to claim the attention of the public, the name of Hayyim N. Bialik [1] ought to be mentioned, a vigorous lyricist and an incomparable stylist, and of S. Tchernichovski, [2] an erotic poet, the singer of love and beauty, a Hebrew with an Hellenic soul. [Footnote 1: Poems published at Warsaw In 1902.] [Footnote 2: Poems published at Warsaw in 1900-2.] These two, both of them at the beginning of their career, are the most brilliant in a group of poets more or less well known.

Again, there are two story-writers that are particularly prominent, Abramowitsch, the old favorite, who, having abandoned Hebrew for a brief period in favor of jargon, returned to enrich Hebrew literature with a series of tales, poetic and humorous, of incomparable originality and in a style all his own. [Collected Tales and Novels, Odessa, 1900.] The second one is Isaac Lob Perez, the symbolist painter of love and misery, a charming teller of tales and a distinguished artist. [Works, in ten volumes, Hebrew Library of ***Tushiyah***, 1899-1901.]

Of novelists and romancers, in prose and in verse, Samuely may be mentioned, and Goldin, Berschadsky, Feierberg, J. Kahn, Berditchevsky, S. L. Gordon, N. Pines, Rabinovitz, Steinberg, and Loubochitzky, to name only a few among many. Ben-

Avigdor is the creator of the young realist movement, through his psychologic tales of ghetto life, particularly his *Menahem ha-Sofer* ("Menahem the Scribe"), wherein he opposes the new chauvinism.

Among the masters of the *feuilleton* are the subtle critic David Frischmann, translator of numerous scientific books; the writer of charming *causeries*, A. L. Levinski, author of a Zionist Utopia, "Journey to Palestine in the Year 5800", published in *Ha-Pardes* ("Paradise"), in Odessa; and J. H. Taviow, the witty writer.

On the field of thought and criticism, the most prominent place belongs to Ahad ha-'Am, the first editor of the review *Ha-Shiloah*, a critic who often drops into paradoxes, but is always original and bold. [Collected Essays, published at Odessa in 1885, and at Warsaw in 1901.] He is the promoter of "spiritual Zionism", the counterstroke dealt to the practical, political movement by Messianic mysticism clothed in a somewhat more rational garb than its traditional form. He has a fine critical mind and is an acute observer, as well as a remarkable stylist.

To Ahad ha-'Am we may oppose Wolf Jawitz, the philosopher of religious romanticism, the defender of tradition, and one of the regenerators of Hebrew style. [*Ha-Arez*, published at Jerusalem in 1893-96; "History of the Jews", published at Wilna, 1898-1902, etc.] Between these two extremes, there is a moderate party, the foremost representative of which is Nahum Sokolow, the popular and prolific editor of *Ha-Zefirah*, prominent at once as a writer and a man of action. Dr. S. Bernfeld also deserves mention, as the admirable popularizer of the Science of Judaism, and an excellent historian, the author of a history of Jewish theology recently published at Warsaw.

Among the latest claimants of public attention is M. J. Berditchevsky, author of numerous tales bordering upon the decadent, but not wholly bare of the spirit of poetry. David Neumark takes rank as a thinker. Philology is worthily represented by Joshua Steinberg, author of a scientific grammar on original lines, not yet known to the scholars of Europe, and translator of the Sibylline books. [*Ma'arke Leshon Eber* ("The Principles of the Hebrew Language"), Wilna, 1884, etc.] Fabius Mises has published a history of modern philosophy in Europe, and J. L. Katzenelenson is the author of a treatise on anatomy and of a number of literary works acceptable to the public. Then there are Leon Rabinovich, editor of *Ha-Meliz*, David Yellin,

Lerner, A. Kahana, and others.

The history of modern literature has found a worthy representative in the person of Reuben Brainin, a master of style, himself the author of popular tales. His remarkable studies of Mapu, Smolenskin, and other writers, are conceived and executed according to the approved methods of modern critics. They have done good work in refining the taste and aesthetic feeling of the Hebrew-reading public.

All these, and a number of others, have given the Hebrew language an assured place. To their original works must be added numberless translations, text books, and editions of all sorts, and then we can form a fair idea of the actual significance of Hebrew in its modern development. In the number of publications, it ranks as the third literature in Russia, the Russian and the Polish being the only ones ahead of it, and no estimate of the influence it wields can afford to leave out of account its vogue in Palestine, Austria, and America.

CONCLUSION

A glance at modern Hebrew literature as a whole reveals a striking tendency in its development, at once unexpected and inevitable. The humanist ideal, which stood sponsor at its rebirth, bore within itself a germ of dissolution. For national and religious aims it desired to substitute the idea of liberty and equality. Sooner or later it would have had to end in assimilation. During the course of a whole century, from the appearance of the first issue of ***Ha-Meassef***, in 1784-5, until the cessation of ***Ha-Shahar***, in 1885, Hebrew literature offers the spectacle of a constant conflict between the humanist ideals and Judaism. In spite of obstacles of every kind, and in spite of the dangerous rivalry of the European languages, the rivalry of the Jewish- German itself, the Hebrew language has given proof of persistent vitality, and displayed surprising power of adaptation to all sorts of circumstances and all departments of literature, and widely separated countries have been the scene of its development. So far as the earliest humanists had planned, the Hebrew language was to serve only as an instrument of propaganda and emancipation. Thanks to the efforts of Moses Hayyim Luzzatto, Mendes, and Wessely, it rose for a brief moment to the rank of a truly literary medium, very soon, however, to make way for the languages of the various countries, while it receded to the narrow confines provided by the Maskilim. Its final destiny was to be decided in Slav lands. In Galicia, it gave birth, in the domain of philosophy, to the ideal of the "mission of the Jewish people", and to the "science of Judaism." But for the great mass of the Jews remaining faithful to the Messianic ideal, what was of greatest significance was the national and religious romanticism expounded by Samuel David Luzzatto.

Lithuania, with its inexhaustible resources, moral and intellectual, became the stronghold of Hebrew. In its double aspect as a humanistic and a romantic force,

Hebrew literature bounded forward on new paths with the lustiness of youth. Before long, under the impetus of social and economic reforms, the Hebrew writers declared war upon a Rabbinical authority that rejected every innovation, and was opposed to all progress. To meet the issue, the realistic literature came forward, polemic and destructive in character. A pitiless combat ensued between the humanists and Rabbinism, and the consequences were fateful for the one party as well as the other. Rabbinism felt that its very essence had been shaken, and that it was destined to disappear, at least in its traditional form. Humanism, on the other side, startled out of its dreams of justice and equality, lost ground, inch by inch, by reason of having broken with the national hope of the people. The attempt made by some writers to bring about the harmonization of religion and life turned out a lamentable miscarriage. The antagonism between the literary folk and the mass of believers ended in the breaking up of the whole literature created by the humanists. At that moment the progressive national movement made its appearance with Smolenskin, and supplied Hebrew literature with a purpose and its civilizing mission.

The predominant note of contemporary Hebrew literature is the Zionist ideal stripped of its mystical envelopes. It may be asserted that the Messianic hope in this new form is in the act of producing a transformation in Polish Hasidic surroundings, identical with that achieved by humanism in Lithuania. The rabid opposition offered to Hebrew literature by the Hasidim suffices to confirm this prognostication of a dreaded result.

Also beyond the boundaries of the Slav countries, in the distant Orient, the Hebrew lion is gaining territory, from Palestine to Morocco, and wherever his foot treads, culture springs up and national regeneration.

* * * * *

Deep down in the sorely tried soul of the Jewish masses, there reposes a fund of idealism, and ardent faith in a better future unshaken by time or disappointments. Defraud them of the millennial ideal which sustains their courage, which is the very cornerstone of their existence, and you surrender them into the power of a dangerous despair, you push them into the arms of the demoralization that lies in wait everywhere, and in some countries has already come out in the open.

Hebrew literature, faithful to its Biblical mission, has within it the power of replenishing the moral resources of the masses and making their hearts thrill with enthusiasm for justice and the ideal. It is the focus of the rays vivifying all that breathes, that struggles, that creates, that hopes within the Jewish soul.

To misunderstand this moral bearing of the renascence of the Hebrew language is to fail to know the very life of the better part of Judaism and the Jew.

* * * * *

Literary creation is now at its full blossom, and the ferment of ideas instilled from all sides is so powerful that an abundant harvest may be expected.

And that Bible language which has given humanity so many glorious pages, which has but now, thanks to the humanists, added a new page, is it destined in very truth to be born anew, and become once more the language of the national culture of the whole of the Jewish people? It would be rash to reply with a categorical affirmative.

What has been proved in the foregoing pages is, we believe, that it exists, and is developing both as a literary and a spoken language; that it has shown itself to be the equal of the modern languages; that it is capable of giving expression to all thoughts and all forms of human activity; and, finally, that it is accomplishing a work of culture and emancipation. The expansion of the language of the prophets taking place under our eyes is a fact that cannot but fascinate every mind interested in the mysterious evolution of the destinies of mankind in the direction of the ideal.

www.bookjungle.com *email: sales@bookjungle.com fax: 630-214-0564 mail: Book Jungle PO Box 2226 Champaign, IL 61825*

The Codes Of Hammurabi And Moses
W. W. Davies

QTY

The discovery of the Hammurabi Code is one of the greatest achievements of archaeology, and is of paramount interest, not only to the student of the Bible, but also to all those interested in ancient history...

Religion   **ISBN:** *1-59462-338-4*   **Pages:** 132
MSRP $12.95

The Theory of Moral Sentiments
Adam Smith

QTY

This work from 1749. contains original theories of conscience amd moral judgment and it is the foundation for systemof morals.

Philosophy   **ISBN:** *1-59462-777-0*   **Pages:** 536
MSRP $19.95

Jessica's First Prayer
Hesba Stretton

QTY

In a screened and secluded corner of one of the many railway-bridges which span the streets of London there could be seen a few years ago, from five o'clock every morning until half past eight, a tidily set-out coffee-stall, consisting of a trestle and board, upon which stood two large tin cans, with a small fire of charcoal burning under each so as to keep the coffee boiling during the early hours of the morning when the work-people were thronging into the city on their way to their daily toil...

Childrens   **ISBN:** *1-59462-373-2*   **Pages:** 84
MSRP $9.95

My Life and Work
Henry Ford

QTY

Henry Ford revolutionized the world with his implementation of mass production for the Model T automobile. Gain valuable business insight into his life and work with his own auto-biography... "We have only started on our development of our country we have not as yet, with all our talk of wonderful progress, done more than scratch the surface. The progress has been wonderful enough but..."

Biographies/   **ISBN:** *1-59462-198-5*   **Pages:** 300
MSRP $21.95

www.bookjungle.com *email: sales@bookjungle.com fax: 630-214-0564 mail: Book Jungle PO Box 2226 Champaign, IL 61825*

The Art of Cross-Examination
Francis Wellman

QTY

I presume it is the experience of every author, after his first book is published upon an important subject, to be almost overwhelmed with a wealth of ideas and illustrations which could readily have been included in his book, and which to his own mind, at least, seem to make a second edition inevitable. Such certainly was the case with me; and when the first edition had reached its sixth impression in five months, I rejoiced to learn that it seemed to my publishers that the book had met with a sufficiently favorable reception to justify a second and considerably enlarged edition. ..

Reference   ISBN: *1-59462-647-2*   Pages:412   MSRP *$19.95*

On the Duty of Civil Disobedience
Henry David Thoreau

QTY

Thoreau wrote his famous essay, On the Duty of Civil Disobedience, as a protest against an unjust but popular war and the immoral but popular institution of slave-owning. He did more than write—he declined to pay his taxes, and was hauled off to gaol in consequence. Who can say how much this refusal of his hastened the end of the war and of slavery ?

Law   ISBN: *1-59462-747-9*   Pages:48   MSRP *$7.45*

Dream Psychology Psychoanalysis for Beginners
Sigmund Freud

QTY

Sigmund Freud, born Sigismund Schlomo Freud (May 6, 1856 - September 23, 1939), was a Jewish-Austrian neurologist and psychiatrist who co-founded the psychoanalytic school of psychology. Freud is best known for his theories of the unconscious mind, especially involving the mechanism of repression; his redefinition of sexual desire as mobile and directed towards a wide variety of objects; and his therapeutic techniques, especially his understanding of transference in the therapeutic relationship and the presumed value of dreams as sources of insight into unconscious desires.

Psychology   ISBN: *1-59462-905-6*   Pages:196   MSRP *$15.45*

The Miracle of Right Thought
Orison Swett Marden

QTY

Believe with all of your heart that you will do what you were made to do. When the mind has once formed the habit of holding cheerful, happy, prosperous pictures, it will not be easy to form the opposite habit. It does not matter how improbable or how far away this realization may see, or how dark the prospects may be, if we visualize them as best we can, as vividly as possible, hold tenaciously to them and vigorously struggle to attain them, they will gradually become actualized, realized in the life. But a desire, a longing without endeavor, a yearning abandoned or held indifferently will vanish without realization.

Self Help   ISBN: *1-59462-644-8*   Pages:360   MSRP *$25.45*

www.bookjungle.com email: sales@bookjungle.com fax: 630-214-0564 mail: Book Jungle PO Box 2226 Champaign, IL 61825

QTY

	Title	ISBN	Price
☐	**The Rosicrucian Cosmo-Conception Mystic Christianity** by *Max Heindel*	ISBN: 1-59462-188-8	$38.95
	The Rosicrucian Cosmo-conception is not dogmatic, neither does it appeal to any other authority than the reason of the student. It is: not controversial, but is: sent forth in the, hope that it may help to clear...	New Age/Religion Pages 646	
☐	**Abandonment To Divine Providence** by *Jean-Pierre de Caussade*	ISBN: 1-59462-228-0	$25.95
	"The Rev. Jean Pierre de Caussade was one of the most remarkable spiritual writers of the Society of Jesus in France in the 18th Century. His death took place at Toulouse in 1751. His works have gone through many editions and have been republished...	Inspirational/Religion Pages 400	
☐	**Mental Chemistry** by *Charles Haanel*	ISBN: 1-59462-192-6	$23.95
	Mental Chemistry allows the change of material conditions by combining and appropriately utilizing the power of the mind. Much like applied chemistry creates something new and unique out of careful combinations of chemicals the mastery of mental chemistry...	New Age Pages 354	
☐	**The Letters of Robert Browning and Elizabeth Barret Barrett 1845-1846 vol II** by *Robert Browning* and *Elizabeth Barrett*	ISBN: 1-59462-193-4	$35.95
		Biographies Pages 596	
☐	**Gleanings In Genesis (volume I)** by *Arthur W. Pink*	ISBN: 1-59462-130-6	$27.45
	Appropriately has Genesis been termed "the seed plot of the Bible" for in it we have, in germ form, almost all of the great doctrines which are afterwards fully developed in the books of Scripture which follow...	Religion/Inspirational Pages 420	
☐	**The Master Key** by *L. W. de Laurence*	ISBN: 1-59462-001-6	$30.95
	In no branch of human knowledge has there been a more lively increase of the spirit of research during the past few years than in the study of Psychology, Concentration and Mental Discipline. The requests for authentic lessons in Thought Control, Mental Discipline and...	New Age/Business Pages 422	
☐	**The Lesser Key Of Solomon Goetia** by *L. W. de Laurence*	ISBN: 1-59462-092-X	$9.95
	This translation of the first book of the "Lernegton" which is now for the first time made accessible to students of Talismanic Magic was done, after careful collation and edition, from numerous Ancient Manuscripts in Hebrew, Latin, and French...	New Age/Occult Pages 92	
☐	**Rubaiyat Of Omar Khayyam** by *Edward Fitzgerald*	ISBN: 1-59462-332-5	$13.95
	Edward Fitzgerald, whom the world has already learned, in spite of his own efforts to remain within the shadow of anonymity, to look upon as one of the rarest poets of the century, was born at Bredfield, in Suffolk, on the 31st of March, 1809. He was the third son of John Purcell...	Music Pages 172	
☐	**Ancient Law** by *Henry Maine*	ISBN: 1-59462-128-4	$29.95
	The chief object of the following pages is to indicate some of the earliest ideas of mankind, as they are reflected in Ancient Law, and to point out the relation of those ideas to modern thought.	Religiom/History Pages 452	
☐	**Far-Away Stories** by *William J. Locke*	ISBN: 1-59462-129-2	$19.45
	"Good wine needs no bush, but a collection of mixed vintages does. And this book is just such a collection. Some of the stories I do not want to remain buried for ever in the museum files of dead magazine-numbers an author's not unpardonable vanity..."	Fiction Pages 272	
☐	**Life of David Crockett** by *David Crockett*	ISBN: 1-59462-250-7	$27.45
	"Colonel David Crockett was one of the most remarkable men of the times in which he lived. Born in humble life, but gifted with a strong will, an indomitable courage, and unremitting perseverance...	Biographies/New Age Pages 424	
☐	**Lip-Reading** by *Edward Nitchie*	ISBN: 1-59462-206-X	$25.95
	Edward B. Nitchie, founder of the New York School for the Hard of Hearing, now the Nitchie School of Lip-Reading, Inc, wrote "LIP-READING Principles and Practice". The development and perfecting of this meritorious work on lip-reading was an undertaking...	How-to Pages 400	
☐	**A Handbook of Suggestive Therapeutics, Applied Hypnotism, Psychic Science** by *Henry Munro*	ISBN: 1-59462-214-0	$24.95
		Health/New Age/Health/Self-help Pages 376	
☐	**A Doll's House: and Two Other Plays** by *Henrik Ibsen*	ISBN: 1-59462-112-8	$19.95
	Henrik Ibsen created this classic when in revolutionary 1848 Rome. Introducing some striking concepts in playwriting for the realist genre, this play has been studied the world over.	Fiction Classics/Plays 308	
☐	**The Light of Asia** by *sir Edwin Arnold*	ISBN: 1-59462-204-3	$13.95
	In this poetic masterpiece, Edwin Arnold describes the life and teachings of Buddha. The man who was to become known as Buddha to the world was born as Prince Gautama of India but he rejected the worldly riches and abandoned the reigns of power when...	Religion/History/Biographies Pages 170	
☐	**The Complete Works of Guy de Maupassant** by *Guy de Maupassant*	ISBN: 1-59462-157-8	$16.95
	"For days and days, nights and nights, I had dreamed of that first kiss which was to consecrate our engagement, and I knew not on what spot I should put my lips..."	Fiction/Classics Pages 240	
☐	**The Art of Cross-Examination** by *Francis L. Wellman*	ISBN: 1-59462-309-0	$26.95
	Written by a renowned trial lawyer, Wellman imparts his experience and uses case studies to explain how to use psychology to extract desired information through questioning.	How-to/Science/Reference Pages 408	
☐	**Answered or Unanswered?** by *Louisa Vaughan* Miracles of Faith in China	ISBN: 1-59462-248-5	$10.95
		Religion Pages 112	
☐	**The Edinburgh Lectures on Mental Science (1909)** by *Thomas*	ISBN: 1-59462-008-3	$11.95
	This book contains the substance of a course of lectures recently given by the writer in the Queen Street Hall, Edinburgh. Its purpose is to indicate the Natural Principles governing the relation between Mental Action and Material Conditions...	New Age/Psychology Pages 148	
☐	**Ayesha** by *H. Rider Haggard*	ISBN: 1-59462-301-5	$24.95
	Verily and indeed it is the unexpected that happens! Probably if there was one person upon the earth from whom the Editor of this, and of a certain previous history, did not expect to hear again...	Classics Pages 380	
☐	**Ayala's Angel** by *Anthony Trollope*	ISBN: 1-59462-352-X	$29.95
	The two girls were both pretty, but Lucy who was twenty-one who supposed to be simple and comparatively unattractive, whereas Ayala was credited, as her Bombwhat romantic name might show, with poetic charm and a taste for romance. Ayala when her father died was nineteen...	Fiction Pages 484	
☐	**The American Commonwealth** by *James Bryce*	ISBN: 1-59462-286-8	$34.45
	An interpretation of American democratic political theory. It examines political mechanics and society from the perspective of Scotsman James Bryce	Politics Pages 572	
☐	**Stories of the Pilgrims** by *Margaret P. Pumphrey*	ISBN: 1-59462-116-0	$17.95
	This book explores pilgrims religious oppression in England as well as their escape to Holland and eventual crossing to America on the Mayflower, and their early days in New England...	History Pages 268	

www.bookjungle.com email: sales@bookjungle.com fax: 630-214-0564 mail: Book Jungle PO Box 2226 Champaign, IL 61825

QTY

The Fasting Cure *by Sinclair Upton* ISBN: *1-59462-222-1* $13.95
In the Cosmopolitan Magazine for May, 1910, and in the Contemporary Review (London) for April, 1910, I published an article dealing with my experiences in fasting. I have written a great many magazine articles, but never one which attracted so much attention... *New Age/Self Help/Health Pages 164*

Hebrew Astrology *by Sepharial* ISBN: *1-59462-308-2* $13.45
In these days of advanced thinking it is a matter of common observation that we have left many of the old landmarks behind and that we are now pressing forward to greater heights and to a wider horizon than that which represented the mind-content of our progenitors... *Astrology Pages 144*

Thought Vibration or The Law of Attraction in the Thought World ISBN: *1-59462-127-6* $12.95
by William Walker Atkinson *Psychology/Religion Pages 144*

Optimism *by Helen Keller* ISBN: *1-59462-108-X* $15.95
Helen Keller was blind, deaf, and mute since 19 months old, yet famously learned how to overcome these handicaps, communicate with the world, and spread her lectures promoting optimism. An inspiring read for everyone... *Biographies/Inspirational Pages 84*

Sara Crewe *by Frances Burnett* ISBN: *1-59462-360-0* $9.45
In the first place, Miss Minchin lived in London. Her home was a large, dull, tall one, in a large, dull square, where all the houses were alike, and all the sparrows were alike, and where all the door-knockers made the same heavy sound... *Childrens/Classic Pages 88*

The Autobiography of Benjamin Franklin *by Benjamin Franklin* ISBN: *1-59462-135-7* $24.95
The Autobiography of Benjamin Franklin has probably been more extensively read than any other American historical work, and no other book of its kind has had such ups and downs of fortune. Franklin lived for many years in England, where he was agent... *Biographies/History Pages 332*

Name	
Email	
Telephone	
Address	
City, State ZIP	

☐ Credit Card   ☐ Check / Money Order

Credit Card Number	
Expiration Date	
Signature	

Please Mail to: Book Jungle
                   PO Box 2226
                   Champaign, IL 61825
or Fax to: 630-214-0564

ORDERING INFORMATION

web: *www.bookjungle.com*
email: *sales@bookjungle.com*
fax: *630-214-0564*
mail: *Book Jungle PO Box 2226 Champaign, IL 61825*
or PayPal *to sales@bookjungle.com*

Please contact us for bulk discounts

DIRECT-ORDER TERMS

**20% Discount if You Order
Two or More Books**
Free Domestic Shipping!
Accepted: Master Card, Visa,
Discover, American Express

www.ingramcontent.com/pod-product-compliance
Lightning Source LLC
Chambersburg PA
CBHW080507110426
42742CB00017B/3028